Company's Coming®

PIZZA !

by
Jean Paré

Dedication

Pizza—great taste any way you slice it!

Cover Photo

1. Blackened Chicken Pizza, page 66
   (on Basic Pizza Crust)
2. Veggie Salad Pizza, page 149
   (on Biscuit Pizza Crust)
3. Pepperoni Solo Pizza, page 70
   (on Confetti Biscuit Pizza Crust)
4. Thai Goodness Pizza, page 56
   (on Basic Pizza Crust)
5. Fruit Pizza, page 80

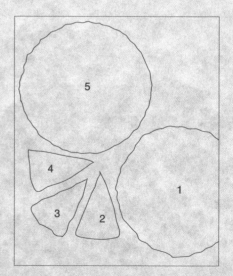

PIZZA!

Second Printing March 1999

Canadian Cataloguing in Publication Data

Paré, Jean
Pizza!

Issued also in French under title: Les pizzas!
Includes index.
ISBN 1-895455-52-9

1. Pizza. I. Title.

TX770.P58P37 1999   641.8'24   C98-901019-8

Published and Distributed by
Company's Coming Publishing Limited
2311 - 96 Street
Edmonton, Alberta, Canada
T6N 1G3

**Published Simultaneously in
Canada and the United States of America**

Printed In Canada

Company's Coming Cookbooks
by Jean Paré

table of Contents

the Jean Paré story

Jean Paré grew up understanding that the combination of family, friends and home cooking is the essence of a good life. From her mother she learned to appreciate good cooking, while her father praised even her earliest attempts. When she left home she took with her many acquired family recipes, her love of cooking and her intriguing desire to read recipe books like novels!

In 1963, when her four children had all reached school age, Jean volunteered to cater to the 50th anniversary of the Vermilion School of Agriculture, now Lakeland College. Working out of her home, Jean prepared a dinner for over 1000 people which launched a flourishing catering operation that continued for over eighteen years. During that time she was provided with countless opportunities to test new ideas with immediate feedback—resulting in empty plates and contented customers! Whether preparing cocktail sandwiches for a house party or serving a hot meal for 1500 people, Jean Paré earned a reputation for good food, courteous service and reasonable prices.

"Why don't you write a cookbook?" Time and again, as requests for her recipes mounted, Jean was asked that question. Jean's response was to team up with her son, Grant Lovig, in the fall of 1980 to form Company's Coming Publishing Limited. April 14, 1981, marked the debut of "150 DELICIOUS SQUARES", the first Company's Coming cookbook in what soon would become Canada's most popular cookbook series.

Jean Paré's operation has grown steadily from the early days of working out of a spare bedroom in her home. Full-time staff includes marketing personnel located in major cities across Canada. Home Office is based in Edmonton, Alberta in a modern building constructed specially for the company.

Today the company distributes throughout Canada and the United States in addition to numerous overseas markets, all under the guidance of Jean's daughter, Gail Lovig. Best-sellers many times over, Company's Coming cookbooks are published in English and French, plus a Spanish-language edition is available in Mexico. Familiar and trusted in home kitchens the world over, Company's Coming cookbooks are offered in a variety of formats, including the original softcover series.

Jean Paré's approach to cooking has always called for quick and easy recipes using everyday ingredients. Even when travelling, she is constantly on the lookout for new ideas to share with her readers. At home, she can usually be found researching and writing recipes, or working in the company's test kitchen. Jean continues to gain new supporters by adhering to what she calls "the golden rule of cooking": never share a recipe you wouldn't use yourself. It's an approach that works—*millions of times over!*

Foreword

The first pizza is believed to have been created in Naples, Italy, about 1000 years ago. It didn't really become popular in North America until after World War II when armed forces stationed in Italy brought home their love of pizza. In the years that followed there was an explosion of pizza outlets, offering an ever-increasing variety of toppings. Today pizza has become more than just a popular food for kids—it's a quick and delicious meal enjoyed equally by all ages.

Pizza can often contain all 4 food groups—dairy, vegetable, meat (or meat substitute) and grains, depending on the crust, sauce and toppings you choose. The amount of fat will vary with the type and amount of cheese and meat used; the best way to control fat content is to make your own pizza! After you see how easy it is, you will be freezing crusts, ready for assembling at a moment's notice. (See Freezing Crusts, page 8.) You may want to compare a thin crust and thick crust to find your favorite. Try yeast crusts that have been risen, and then try again without allowing them to rise. If you don't have any partially baked crusts ready in the freezer, buy some at your local supermarket. If time is short, make a biscuit crust.

Why serve pizza? It's fun to eat, tastes good, is easy, quick, and inexpensive. It can be eaten out of the hand and rarely requires a knife and fork. You can eat it sitting down or standing up. It's even great the next day, served either cold or reheated in the microwave. Pizza is so versatile that you can make appetizers, breakfasts, snacks, main courses, side dishes, salads and desserts. From small to large, round to square, double crust to calzones, before long, if you aren't already, you will become a serious pizza lover.

Serve Savory Pizza Tarts as an appetizer. Chicken Fiesta Pizza makes a great main course. And you must try Baked Alaska Pizza for dessert! For a real entertaining change, host a Pizza Party. We've included some suggestions on page 9, but add your own ideas and creativity. Get ready—Company's Coming is delivering PIZZA!

Jean Paré

Each recipe has been analyzed using the most updated version of the Canadian Nutrient File from Health And Welfare Canada which is based upon the United States Department of Agriculture (USDA) Nutrient Data Base.

Margaret Ng, B.Sc. (Hon), M.A., Registered Dietician

CRUSTS

A regular 12 inch (30 cm) crust uses 2 cups (500 mL) of flour. For a thinner crust, reduce to 1½ cups (375 mL) of flour. Extra fat produces a softer crust, while less fat makes a drier and more chewy crust.

a) Biscuit Crust: These are quick, easy to make and do not require any rising time.

b) Yeast Crust: Yeast crusts (whether made with active dry or instant yeast) can be mixed, kneaded and formed right in the pizza pan—what a time-saver! Active dry yeast does not necessarily need to be proofed (dissolved) in water first but can instead be added directly to the dry mixture as long as very warm liquid is used. The majority of crust recipes in this book were tested using the traditional method of allowing dough to rise once in the bowl and then again in the pan. A yeast crust that has been allowed to rise in the pan in a warm place for 20 minutes will produce a thicker crust.

Cornmeal Bottom: Cornmeal on the bottom of a crust adds a crispy texture and enhances the flavor. Grease the pizza pan and sprinkle with about 1 to 2 tbsp. (15 to 30 mL) cornmeal. Roll out and stretch dough to the size of your pan before placing it, otherwise the dough will slip all over the cornmeal.

Freezing Pizza Crusts: Prepare crusts. (See Partially Baked Crusts, below.) Cool completely. Freeze in plastic bag, placing waxed paper in between each crust if freezing several at a time.

Partially Baked Crusts: Prepare dough. Roll out and press in greased 12 inch (30 cm) pizza pan, forming a rim around edge. If using a yeast crust, poke holes all over with a fork. Bake on bottom rack in 425°F (220°C) oven for 4 to 5 minutes. Press down any bulges, using a tea towel to protect your fingers from heat. If using a biscuit crust do not poke holes. And, remember, toppings will have less time to cook on a partially baked crust.

EQUIPMENT

Pizza Cutters: A good-size cutting wheel makes cutting pizza a breeze. Scissors also work well. For easiest cutting, push baked (and partially cooled) pizza off the pan onto a cutting board. This allows you to cut straight down instead of having to avoid the edge, and keeps the baking pan from becoming damaged. For dessert pizzas, first line the pan with foil, because crumb crusts are difficult to push off without breaking. Just pull foil with pizza from pan to cutting board.

Pizza Pan Holders: A pan holder clamps onto a hot pizza pan to remove it from the oven. Pot holders or oven mitts can break the crust or become dirty from touching the topping.

Pizza Pans: Recipes were tested using dark, non-stick 12 inch (30 cm) pizza pans, producing a crispier crust than lighter pans. Most of the pizzas in this book were baked in a preheated 425°F (220°C) oven. For a crispier crust, bake pizzas on the bottom rack in the oven, unless stated otherwise. Pizza pans with holes all over the bottom are great for reheating, or for creating crispy bottoms on partially baked crusts. The majority of crust recipes throughout Pizza! make enough dough to fit a 12 inch (30 cm) round pizza pan. If you choose to use a different pan size, refer to this chart.

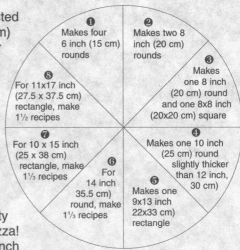

The dough for a 12 inch (30 cm) pan can be used to make pizzas on different sizes of pans as noted above (1 through 6). Use more dough for larger pans (7 or 8)

In the diagram:
- ❶ Makes four 6 inch (15 cm) rounds
- ❷ Makes two 8 inch (20 cm) rounds
- ❸ Makes one 8 inch (20 cm) round and one 8x8 inch (20x20 cm) square
- ❹ Makes one 10 inch (25 cm) round slightly thicker than 12 inch, 30 cm)
- ❺ Makes one 9x13 inch 22x33 cm) rectangle
- ❻ For 14 inch 35.5 cm) round, make 1⅓ recipes
- ❼ For 10 x 15 inch (25 x 38 cm) rectangle, make 1⅓ recipes
- ❽ For 11x17 inch (27.5 x 37.5 cm) rectangle, make 1½ recipes

TOPPINGS

Cheeses: The common cheeses used are mozzarella, Cheddar, Parmesan, provolone and Monterey Jack. Edam, asiago, and feta are also used. On a 12 inch (30 cm) pizza, 1½ cups (375 mL) grated cheese is sufficient. Use up to 2 cups (500 mL) if you prefer.

Meats: You may choose just about any kind of meat, but it cannot be raw. There is not enough cooking time to cook raw steak, ground beef, pork, chicken, fish or seafood safely or completely. Precook before adding to pizza. Deli meats work very well on pizza and can be thick-sliced, shaved thin, chopped or sliced. Be careful to not leave pizzas containing meat sitting out too long after serving.

Vegetables: Some vegetables can be added fresh (such as mushrooms or tomato) while others are better if lightly steamed first (such as broccoli, carrot and onion).

PIZZA PARTY

Saturday evening is a great time to host a pizza party. Have enough pre-made balls of pizza dough for at least one per guest, and if needed, ask each guest to bring their own pizza pans. Line up as many toppings as you can in separate bowls on the counter and let creativity begin! For those who are having difficulty deciding on what kind of pizza to make, encourage them to try different toppings on each half of their pizza. Only 2 pizzas can be baked at one time, so have damp tea towels ready to cover the "pizzas-in-waiting". As added fun, try stretching the pizza dough over your fists and tossing it in the air (like at a pizzeria). Remember to keep extra dough handy in case some accidentally land on the floor.

TINY CRAB PIZZAS

Cut into wedges for an appetizer, or serve in one piece for a snack.

English muffins (or hamburger buns), split	4	4
Canned crabmeat, drained and cartilage removed, flaked	4 oz.	113 g
Onion flakes	1 tbsp.	15 mL
Grated sharp Cheddar cheese	1 cup	250 mL
Light salad dressing (or mayonnaise)	2 tbsp.	30 mL
Salt	1/4 tsp.	1 mL
Pepper	1/8 tsp.	0.5 mL
Paprika, sprinkle		
Pimiento-stuffed green olives, sliced (or 32 slices of cherry tomatoes or 8 slices of large tomato)	12	12

Arrange muffin halves on ungreased baking sheet.

Combine next 6 ingredients in small bowl. Mix well. Spread scant 3 tbsp. (50 mL) mixture over each half.

Sprinkle with paprika. Divide olive slices among tops. Bake on center rack in 400°F (205°C) oven for about 10 minutes. Cut each into 4 wedges. Makes 32 appetizers.

1 appetizer: 54 Calories; 3.3 g Total Fat; 402 mg Sodium; 2 g Protein; 4 g Carbohydrate; 1 g Dietary Fiber

Pictured on page 17.

MUFFIN PIZZA APPETIZERS

For a perfect school lunch, leave whole or use mini pitas or bagels.

English muffins, split and toasted (buttered, optional)	4	4
Marinara Pizza Sauce, page 137 (or other)	1/2 cup	125 mL
Thinly sliced pepperoni (small diameter)	4 oz.	113 g
Grated part-skim mozzarella cheese	1 cup	250 mL

(continued on next page)

Arrange muffin halves on ungreased baking sheet.

Spread each half with 1 tbsp. (15 mL) sauce.

Place pepperoni slices over sauce. There should be about 8 pieces on each muffin half. Sprinkle cheese over pepperoni slices. Bake on center rack in 400°F (205°C) oven for about 5 minutes. Cut each into 4 wedges. Makes 32 appetizers.

1 appetizer: 48 Calories; 2.4 g Total Fat; 124 mg Sodium; 2 g Protein; 4 g Carbohydrate; trace Dietary Fiber

Pictured on page 71.

CURRIED CHEESE PILLOWS

Cut these puffy bright yellow little pizzas into small wedges for appetizers or leave whole for snacks. Mild curry flavor. Just right.

Cream cheese, softened	8 oz.	250 g
Grated sharp Cheddar cheese	1 cup	250 mL
Sherry (or alcohol-free sherry)	2 tbsp.	30 mL
Worcestershire sauce	1 tsp.	5 mL
Lemon juice	1 tsp.	5 mL
Curry powder	$\frac{1}{2}$ tsp.	2 mL
Onion powder	$\frac{1}{4}$ tsp.	1 mL
Salt	$\frac{1}{8}$ tsp.	0.5 mL
Pita breads (3 inch, 7.5 cm), or English muffin halves	12	12
Alfalfa sprouts (small handful), optional		

Mix first 8 ingredients well in small bowl. Makes $1\frac{1}{3}$ cups (325 mL) topping.

Poke each pita with fork so it doesn't puff up too much. Spread about 2 tbsp. (30 mL) topping over each pita. Arrange on ungreased baking sheet. Bake on center rack in 425°F (220°C) oven for about 5 minutes.

Scatter alfalfa sprouts over hot rounds. Cut each into 4 wedges. Makes 48 small appetizers.

1 appetizer: 39 Calories; 2.7 g Total Fat; 52 mg Sodium; 1 g Protein; 2 g Carbohydrate; trace Dietary Fiber

COLD SEAFOOD PIZZA

Each wedge reveals luscious layers that promise to be addictive. Very attractive. This pizza can also be made in a 9 x 13 inch (22 x 33 cm) pan. Serve cold.

Partially baked 12 inch (30 cm) pizza crust, your choice, pages 115 to 130 (see Crusts, page 8), or commercial	1	1
Light cream cheese, softened	8 oz.	250 g
Light salad dressing (or mayonnaise)	1/4 cup	60 mL
Non-fat sour cream	1/4 cup	60 mL
Canned small shrimp, drained (or frozen, thawed and cooked)	4 oz.	113 g
Canned crabmeat, drained and cartilage removed (or imitation crabmeat), flaked	4 oz.	113 g
Chopped green onion	2 tbsp.	30 mL
SEAFOOD COCKTAIL SAUCE		
Chili sauce	1/3 cup	75 mL
Ketchup	1/4 cup	60 mL
Sweet pickle relish	2 tbsp.	30 mL
Prepared horseradish	1 tsp.	5 mL
Worcestershire sauce	1/4 tsp.	1 mL
Onion powder	1/8 tsp.	0.5 mL
Grated part-skim mozzarella cheese	3/4 cup	175 mL
Grated medium Cheddar cheese	3/4 cup	175 mL

Place partially baked crust on ungreased 12 inch (30 cm) pizza pan. Bake on bottom rack in 425°F (220°C) oven for 8 minutes until fully cooked. Cool.

Mash cream cheese, salad dressing and sour cream together until smooth. Spread over crust.

Scatter shrimp, crabmeat and green onion over top.

Seafood Cocktail Sauce: Measure all 6 ingredients into small bowl. Stir together well. Spoon dabs here and there over top of seafood. Spread.

Toss both cheeses together in medium bowl. Sprinkle over all. Chill. Cuts into 16 wedges.

1 wedge: 174 Calories; 7.6 g Total Fat; 460 mg Sodium; 9 g Protein; 17 g Carbohydrate; 1 g Dietary Fiber

SMOKED SALMON PIZZA

Make topping and crust ahead and assemble when needed. A dark crust complements the color of salmon.

Pumpernickel Pizza Crust dough, page 118 (or Rye Pizza Crust dough, page 124)	1	1
Cream cheese, softened	4 oz.	125 g
Lemon juice	1 tsp.	5 mL
Prepared horseradish	1 tsp.	5 mL
Seasoning salt	⅛ tsp.	0.5 mL
Onion powder	⅛ tsp.	0.5 mL
Liquid smoke	½ tsp.	2 mL
Canned salmon, drained, skin and round bones removed, flaked (red is best)	7½ oz.	213 g
Grated mozzarella cheese, for garnish		
Dill weed (or parsley flakes or grated part-skim mozzarella cheese), sprinkle (for garnish)		

Prepare pizza dough. Roll out and press in greased 12 inch (30 cm) pizza pan, forming rim around edge. Poke holes all over with fork. Bake on bottom rack in 425°F (220°C) oven for about 15 minutes. Press down any bulges with tea towel while warm. Bake for 5 minutes until fully cooked. Cool.

Mash next 6 ingredients together in small bowl.

Add salmon. Mash together well. Spread over crust.

Sprinkle with mozzarella cheese and dill weed. Cuts into 16 wedges.

1 wedge: 119 Calories; 5.4 g Total Fat; 180 mg Sodium; 5 g Protein; 13 g Carbohydrate; 1 g Dietary Fiber

Pictured on page 17.

SMOKED SALMON TIDBITS: Spread 2 tbsp. (30 mL) salmon mixture, above, over 10 buttered English muffin halves. Garnish. Cut each into 4 pieces. Makes 40 tidbits.

SAVORY PIZZA TARTS

Quaint little nibbles. Make lots for the freezer.

Cooking oil	2 tsp.	10 mL
Chopped onion	1 cup	250 mL
Chopped fresh mushrooms	1 cup	250 mL
Non-fat sour cream	2 tbsp.	30 mL
Ground rosemary	1/8 tsp.	0.5 mL
Frozen dough buns (2 oz., 57 g, each), thawed	8	8
PIZZA SAUCE		
Tomato sauce	3 tbsp.	50 mL
Dried whole oregano	1/8-1/4 tsp.	0.5-1 mL
Onion powder	1/4 tsp.	1 mL
Granulated sugar	1/4 tsp.	1 mL
Salt	1/8 tsp.	0.5 mL
Grated part-skim mozzarella cheese	1/8 cup	125 mL

Combine cooking oil, onion and mushrooms in medium frying pan. Sauté until soft.

Mix sour cream and rosemary in small cup. Add to mushroom mixture. Stir together.

Cut each bun in half. Press each half in greased muffin pan, forming sides.

Pizza Sauce: Mix all 5 ingredients in small cup. Spoon 1/2 tsp. (2 mL) into each muffin cup. Spoon 1 tbsp. (15 mL) mushroom mixture over each bit of sauce.

Top with cheese, using 1 1/2 tsp. (7 mL) for each. Bake on center rack in 425°F (220°C) oven for about 10 minutes. Makes 16 tarts.

1 tart: 97 Calories; 2.6 g Total Fat; 194 mg Sodium; 3 g Protein; 15 g Carbohydrate; 1 g Dietary Fiber

TACO PIZZA SQUARES

One of those great appetizers that you can serve hot and is just as good when it cools.

Cornmeal Pizza Crust dough, page 116	1	1
Canned refried beans with jalapeños	14 oz.	398 mL
Non-fat sour cream	1 cup	250 mL
Mild or medium salsa	¾ cup	175 mL
Grated Monterey Jack cheese	¾ cup	175 mL
Grated medium Cheddar cheese	¾ cup	175 mL
Green onions, chopped	2	2
Chopped pitted ripe olives	¼ cup	60 mL

Prepare pizza dough. Roll out on working surface until slightly larger than 9 x 13 inches (22 x 33 cm). Sprinkle bottom of greased 9 x 13 (22 x 33 cm) pan with cornmeal. See Cornmeal Bottom, page 8. Place dough in pan, forming rim around edge. Poke holes all over with fork. Bake on center rack in 425°F (220°C) oven for 5 minutes. Press down any bulges with tea towel. Bake for about 5 minutes until fully cooked.

Spread refried beans over crust. Spread sour cream over refried beans. Drizzle with salsa.

Toss both cheeses together in small bowl. Sprinkle over salsa.

Scatter green onion and olives over top. Broil 6 inches (15 cm) from heat until cheese is melted, or bake on center rack in 425°F (220°C) oven for about 5 minutes until cheese is melted. Cuts into 24 squares.

1 square: 118 Calories; 4 g Total Fat; 287 mg Sodium; 5 g Protein; 16 g Carbohydrate; 2 g Dietary Fiber

Pictured on page 107.

A bee wrestler uses behold to pin down another bee wrestler.

HAM PIZZA APPETIZERS

Both crust and topping can be ready ahead of time. Assemble shortly before serving cold to prevent sogginess.

Biscuit Pizza Crust dough, page 128 (or partially baked commercial)	1	1
Canned flakes of ham, with liquid, mashed	2 × 6½ oz.	2 × 184 g
Light salad dressing (or mayonnaise)	2 tbsp.	30 mL
Prepared mustard	2 tsp.	10 mL
Pimiento-stuffed green olives, sliced (optional)	8	8

Prepare pizza dough. Roll out and press in greased 12 inch (30 cm) pizza pan, forming rim around edge. Bake on bottom rack in 400°F (205°C) oven for about 15 minutes until fully cooked. Cool. If using partially baked crust, place directly on bottom rack in 400°F (205°C) oven for 2 minutes. Turn crust over. Bake for 2 minutes. Cool.

Combine remaining 4 ingredients in medium bowl. Mix well. Spread over cooled crust. Cuts into 20 thin wedges.

1 wedge: *104 Calories; 4.7 g Total Fat; 307 mg Sodium; 4 g Protein; 11 g Carbohydrate; trace Dietary Fiber*

Pictured on page 17.

1. Cheese Bake Pizza, page 22
   (on Spinach Biscuit Pizza Crust)
2. Ham Pizza Appetizers, page 16
   (on Biscuit Pizza Crust)
3. Smoked Salmon Pizza, page 13
   (on Pumpernickel Pizza Crust)
4. Tiny Crab Pizzas, page 10
5. Tiny Pizzas, page 23

Props Courtesy Of: Stephe Tate Photo
The Basket House

Appetizer Pizzas

CHEESY CRAB PIZZA SQUARES

Crabmeat gives this appetizer pizza delicious flavor.

Refrigerator crescent-style rolls (8 per tube)	8 oz.	235 g
Light cream cheese, softened	4 oz.	125 g
Non-fat sour cream	$\frac{1}{3}$ cup	75 mL
Lemon juice	1 tsp.	5 mL
Prepared horseradish	1 tsp.	5 mL
Salt	$\frac{1}{4}$ tsp.	1 mL
Pepper	$\frac{1}{8}$ tsp.	0.5 mL
Imitation crabmeat, flaked	$1\frac{1}{2}$ cups	375 mL
Grated part-skim mozzarella cheese	$\frac{1}{2}$ cup	125 mL
Grated medium Cheddar cheese	$\frac{1}{2}$ cup	125 mL
Chopped green onion	$\frac{1}{4}$ cup	60 mL

Unroll dough. Press to fit in bottom of greased 9 x 13 inch (22 x 33 cm) pan. Press seams together. Bake on bottom rack in 375°F (190°C) oven for 8 minutes.

Mash next 6 ingredients together in medium bowl. Stir in crabmeat. Spread over crust.

Toss remaining 3 ingredients together in small bowl. Sprinkle over top. Bake on bottom rack in 375°F (190°C) oven for about 15 minutes. Let stand for 5 minutes. Cuts into 24 squares.

1 square: 51 Calories; 3 g Total Fat; 217 mg Sodium; 4 g Protein; 2 g Carbohydrate; trace Dietary Fiber

A dog has to be an expert on trees so he won't bark up the wrong one.

MEXI-APPIES

Flaky crust with lots of tasty toppings. A very fresh flavor.

Refrigerator crescent-style rolls (8 per tube)	8 oz.	235 g
Light cream cheese, softened	4 oz.	125 g
Light salad dressing (or mayonnaise)	1/3 cup	75 mL
Commercial taco sauce (mild or medium)	1/2 cup	125 mL
Small green pepper, chopped	1	1
Medium tomato, chopped	1	1
Chopped green onion	2 tbsp.	30 mL
Canned chopped green chilies, drained	4 oz.	114 mL
Chopped fresh mushrooms	1/2 cup	125 mL
Chopped pitted ripe (or pimiento-stuffed green) olives (optional)	2 tbsp.	30 mL
Grated medium Cheddar cheese	1 cup	250 mL

Unroll dough. Press to fit in greased 9 x 13 inch (22 x 33 cm) baking pan or 12 inch (30 cm) pizza pan. Press seams together. Bake on bottom rack in 375°F (190°C) oven for about 10 minutes until fully cooked. Cool.

Mash cream cheese and salad dressing together. Spread over crust.

Spoon dabs of taco sauce here and there over top. Spread.

Layer remaining 7 ingredients in order given. Chill. Cuts into 24 squares.

1 square: 63 Calories; 4.2 g Total Fat; 236 mg Sodium; 2 g Protein; 4 g Carbohydrate; trace Dietary Fiber

Pictured on page 107.

HALLOWEEN PIZZAS

Kids will have a great time making these. They are very easy and quick. Don't wait for Halloween.

English muffins, split and lightly buttered	4	4
Basic Pizza Sauce, page 132 (or other)	1/2 cup	125 mL
Process Cheddar cheese slices	4	4
Process mozzarella cheese slices	4	4

(continued on next page)

Arrange muffin halves on broiling tray. Broil until cut sides are toasted.

Spread 1 tbsp. (15 mL) sauce over each bun half.

Cut out jack-o'-lantern faces in cheese. Put 1 face on each muffin half. Cut off corners of cheese slices to fit buns if desired. Arrange on ungreased baking sheet. Bake on center rack in 400°F (205°C) oven for about 3 minutes until cheese is slightly melted. Makes 8 small pizzas.

1 pizza: 203 Calories; 11.2 g Total Fat; 613 mg Sodium; 10 g Protein; 16 g Carbohydrate; 1 g Dietary Fiber

Pictured on page 71.

GUACAMOLE PIZZA

Topping may be made ahead and refrigerated. Crust may also be crisped ahead. Assemble when needed. Nippy and flavorful. Best with white-floured crust.

Partially baked 12 inch (30 cm) pizza crust, your choice, pages 115 to 130 (see Crusts, page 8), or commercial	1	1
Ripe avocados, peeled and mashed	2	2
Lemon juice	2 tbsp.	30 mL
Minced onion flakes	1 tbsp.	15 mL
Salt	½ tsp.	2 mL
Garlic powder	¼ tsp.	1 mL
Hot pepper sauce	¼ tsp.	1 mL
Medium tomato, diced	1	1
Grated sharp Cheddar cheese	½ cup	125 mL

Place partially baked crust directly on bottom rack in 400°F (205°C) oven. Bake for 2 minutes. Turn crust over. Bake for 2 minutes. Cool.

Mash avocado and lemon juice together. Add next 4 ingredients. Mash together. Gently fold in tomato. Spread over crust.

Sprinkle with cheese. Cuts into 20 wedges.

1 wedge: 108 Calories; 5.6 g Total Fat; 123 mg Sodium; 3 g Protein; 12 g Carbohydrate; 1 g Dietary Fiber

Pictured on page 107.

CHEESE BAKE PIZZA

Tastes like a fondue you can eat out of your hand. Has a colorful crust. Good hot or cold.

Spinach Biscuit Pizza Crust dough, page 129 (or other biscuit pizza crust dough, pages 128 to 130)	1	1
Large egg	1	1
All-purpose flour	2 tbsp.	30 mL
Grated Gruyère cheese	3 cups	750 mL
White grape juice (or white wine)	1/4 cup	60 mL
Salt	1/2 tsp.	2 mL
Pepper	1/4 tsp.	1 mL
Garlic powder	1/8 tsp.	0.5 mL
Favorite Tomato Pizza Sauce, page 138 (or other)	1/2 cup	125 mL

Prepare pizza dough. Roll out and press in greased 9 x 13 inch (22 x 33 cm) pan, forming rim around edge.

Beat egg and flour together well in medium bowl.

Stir in next 5 ingredients.

Spread sauce over crust. Spoon cheese mixture over sauce. Bake on bottom rack in 350°F (175°C) oven for 15 to 20 minutes. Cuts into 24 squares.

1 square: 124 Calories; 6.6 g Total Fat; 302 mg Sodium; 6 g Protein; 10 g Carbohydrate; 1 g Dietary Fiber

Pictured on page 17.

FAST CHILI PIZZA APPETIZERS

A pleasant nip. This is one you can serve warm. It is just as good when it cools. Baked in a jelly roll pan to make many servings.

Jumbo Pizza Crust dough, page 122	1	1
Light cream cheese, softened	8 oz.	250 g
Grated Monterey Jack cheese	2 cups	500 mL
Cayenne pepper	1/4 tsp.	1 mL
Onion powder	1/4 tsp.	1 mL
Canned chili without meat	14 oz.	398 mL

Prepare pizza dough. Roll out and press in greased 10 x 15 inch (25 x 38 cm) jelly roll pan, forming rim around edge.

Combine next 4 ingredients in large bowl. Mash together.

Add chili. Stir. Spread over crust. Bake on bottom rack in 425°F (220°C) oven for 10 to 15 minutes until crust is browned and topping is sizzling hot. Cool slightly to allow cheese to set before cutting. Cuts into 36 pieces.

1 piece: 97 Calories; 4.7 g Total Fat; 202 mg Sodium; 4 g Protein; 10 g Carbohydrate; 1 g Dietary Fiber

Pictured on page 107.

TINY PIZZAS

You will find these disappear like magic. These are so cute!

Refrigerator country-style biscuits (10 per tube)	12 oz.	340 g
Commercial pizza sauce	10 tsp.	50 mL
Finely chopped pepperoni	½ cup	125 mL
Grated part-skim mozzarella cheese	½ cup	125 mL

Cut each biscuit into quarters. Press each piece in greased mini-muffin pan, forming sides.

Spoon ¼ tsp. (1 mL) sauce into each. Add ½ tsp. (2 mL) pepperoni. Top each with ½ tsp. (2 mL) cheese. Bake in 425°F (220°C) oven for 8 to 9 minutes. Makes 40 pizzas.

1 pizza; 37 Calories; 1.6 g Total Fat; 125 mg Sodium; 1 g Protein; 4 g Carbohydrate; trace Dietary Fiber

Pictured on page 17.

OPTIONAL TOPPING 1
Salsa
Sliced green onion
Grated Monterey Jack cheese
Grated Cheddar cheese

OPTIONAL TOPPING 2
Commercial pizza sauce
Chopped green pepper
Sliced fresh mushrooms
Grated mozzarella cheese

OPTIONAL TOPPING 3
Seafood cocktail sauce
Shrimp
Grated mozzarella cheese
Grated Edam cheese

OPTIONAL TOPPING 4
Chili sauce
Diced cooked bacon
Grated Cheddar cheese

OPTIONAL TOPPING 5
Commercial pizza sauce
Grated Cheddar cheese
Diced jalapeño peppers

NACHO PIZZA

Forever popular. Best served hot or warm.

Refrigerator crescent-style rolls (8 per tube)	8 oz.	235 g
Canned jalapeño bean dip	½ × 10½ oz.	½ × 298 mL
Onion salt	⅛ tsp.	0.5 mL
Garlic salt	⅛ tsp.	0.5 mL
Cayenne pepper	⅛ tsp.	0.5 mL
Grated medium Cheddar cheese	1 cup	250 mL
Broken corn chips	⅔ cup	150 mL
Seeded and diced tomato	½ cup	125 mL
Chopped green onion	¼ cup	60 mL
Grated medium Cheddar cheese	1 cup	250 mL

Unroll dough. Press to fit in greased 12 inch (30 cm) pizza pan. Press seams together, forming rim around edge. Bake in 375°F (190°C) oven for about 6 minutes until just turning golden. Cool.

Mash bean dip, onion salt, garlic salt and cayenne pepper together in small bowl. Spread over crust.

Sprinkle with first amount of cheese and corn chips. Scatter tomato, green onion and second amount of cheese over top. Return to oven. Bake for 10 minutes. Serve warm. Cuts into 16 wedges.

1 wedge: *107 Calories; 7 g Total Fat; 259 mg Sodium; 5 g Protein; 6 g Carbohydrate; 1 g Dietary Fiber*

Pictured on page 107.

A dog wags a tail and a marine tags a whale.

A bit of crunch from the cornmeal crust. Green chilies add a southwestern flavor. A full-meal deal.

CORNMEAL BISCUIT MIX CRUST

Biscuit mix	2 cups	500 mL
Yellow cornmeal	1/3 cup	75 mL
Water	1/2 cup	125 mL
Canned refried beans	14 oz.	398 mL
Lean ground beef	1 lb.	454 g
Chopped onion	1/2 cup	125 mL
Tomato sauce	7 1/2 oz.	213 mL
Canned chopped green chilies, drained	4 oz.	114 mL
Beef bouillon powder	2 tsp.	10 mL
Chili powder	1 tsp.	5 mL
Grated Monterey Jack cheese	1 1/2 cups	375 mL

Cornmeal Biscuit Mix Crust: Combine all 3 ingredients in medium bowl. Stir until soft ball forms. You may need to add 1 tbsp. (15 mL) more water. It should be quite sticky. Using greased hands, press in greased 12 inch (30 cm) pizza pan, forming rim around edge. Bake in 425°F (220°C) oven for 5 minutes.

Spread crust with refried beans.

Scramble-fry ground beef and onion in medium non-stick frying pan until onion is soft and beef is browned. Remove from heat. Drain.

Add tomato sauce, green chilies, bouillon powder and chili powder. Stir together. Spread over refried beans.

Sprinkle cheese over top. Bake on bottom rack in 425°F (220°C) oven for 15 to 20 minutes. Cuts into 8 wedges.

1 wedge: 411 Calories; 16.8 g Total Fat; 1134 mg Sodium; 23 g Protein; 42 g Carbohydrate; 4 g Dietary Fiber

BEEF FLAMBÉ PIZZA

This calls for a partially baked crust so topping doesn't cook too long. Turn out the lights and pour flaming liqueur over the pizza. Best to eat using a knife and fork.

Partially baked 12 inch (30 cm) pizza crust, your choice, pages 115 to 130 (see Crusts, page 8), or commercial	1	1
Cooking oil	1 tsp.	5 mL
Beef tenderloin, cut into strips	¾ lb.	340 g
Basic Pizza Sauce, page 132 (or other)	½ cup	125 mL
Grated part-skim mozzarella cheese	¾ cup	175 mL
Grated Edam cheese	¾ cup	175 mL
Salt, sprinkle		
Pepper, sprinkle		
Green pepper slivers	½ cup	125 mL
Canned sliced peaches, drained (slice extra thick ones)	14 oz.	398 mL
Grand Marnier liqueur, warmed (not hot)	2 tbsp.	30 mL

Place partially baked crust on ungreased 12 inch (30 cm) pizza pan.

Heat cooking oil in medium frying pan. Add beef strips. Sauté for 1 to 2 minutes. Beef will finish cooking in oven. Remove from heat to cool.

Spread sauce over crust. Sprinkle with both cheeses. Arrange beef over cheese. Sprinkle with salt and pepper. Scatter green pepper over beef. Arrange peach slices over top. Bake on bottom rack in 425°F (220°C) oven for 10 to 12 minutes.

Heat Grand Marnier in small saucepan until warm. Ignite with match. Turn off lights. Pour slowly over pizza in circle, about halfway between center and edge. Let flame die. Cuts into 8 wedges.

1 wedge: 321 Calories; 12.5 g Total Fat; 344 mg Sodium; 19 g Protein; 31 g Carbohydrate; 2 g Dietary Fiber

There is something for everyone. If short of one ingredient, double up on another.

Jumbo Pizza Crust dough, page 122	1	1
Cooking oil	1 tsp.	5 mL
Beef filet (or sirloin), cut into thin strips	1/4 lb.	113 g
Chopped onion	1 cup	250 mL
Medium green pepper, chopped	1	1
Bacon slices	6	6
Favorite Tomato Pizza Sauce, page 138 (or other)	1/2 cup	125 mL
Grated part-skim mozzarella cheese	1 cup	250 mL
Thinly sliced pepperoni	1/4 cup	60 mL
Thinly sliced and cut-up salami	1/4 cup	60 mL
Diced cooked ham	1/4 cup	60 mL
Pineapple tidbits, cut smaller	1 cup	250 mL
Cooked fresh (or frozen) shrimp	1/4 lb.	113 g
Small tomato, diced	1	1
Small (or larger, sliced) mushrooms	1/2 cup	125 mL
Pitted ripe olives, sliced	1/3 cup	75 mL
Grated part-skim mozzarella cheese	1 cup	250 mL

Prepare pizza dough. Roll out and press in greased 10 x 15 inch (25 x 38 cm) jelly roll pan, forming rim around edge.

Combine first 4 ingredients in medium frying pan. Sauté until desired degree of doneness is reached. Transfer to small bowl.

Cook bacon in frying pan. Drain well. Cut into 1/2 inch (12 mm) pieces. Add to beef mixture. Stir together.

Spread sauce over crust. Sprinkle with first amount of cheese. Spoon beef mixture evenly over cheese. Scatter next 9 ingredients over cheese in order given. Bake on bottom rack in 425°F (220°C) oven for 15 to 20 minutes. Cuts into 15 pieces.

1 piece: 229 Calories; 9.1 g Total Fat; 419 mg Sodium; 12 g Protein; 24 g Carbohydrate; 2 g Dietary Fiber

S'GETTI AND MEATBALL PIZZA

A novelty crust with a novelty topping. Little meatballs show up through cheese.

SPAGHETTI CRUST

Spaghetti (or vermicelli)	8 oz.	225 g
Boiling water	2½ qts.	2.5 L
Cooking oil (optional)	1 tbsp.	15 mL
Salt	2 tsp.	10 mL
Large egg, fork-beaten	1	1
Milk	½ cup	125 mL
Salt, sprinkle		
Pepper, sprinkle		

TOPPING

Fine dry bread crumbs	2 tbsp.	30 mL
Grated Parmesan cheese	2 tbsp.	30 mL
Salt	¼ tsp.	1 mL
Pepper	1/16 tsp.	0.5 mL
Garlic powder	⅛ tsp.	0.5 mL
Large egg, fork-beaten	1	1
Lean ground beef	6 oz.	170 g
Marinara Pizza Sauce, page 137	½ cup	125 mL
Grated part-skim mozzarella cheese	1½ cups	375 mL

Spaghetti Crust: Cook spaghetti in boiling water, cooking oil and salt in large saucepan for 11 to 13 minutes until tender but firm. Drain. Return spaghetti to saucepan.

Add egg and milk. Stir. Sprinkle with salt and pepper. Mix well. Press in greased 12 inch (30 cm) pizza pan. Cover to keep moist while preparing meatballs.

Topping: Combine first 6 ingredients in medium bowl. Stir together well.

Add ground beef. Mix. Divide in half. Roll each half into thin log. Cut each into 16 pieces. Shape each piece into tiny ball. Arrange on greased baking sheet with sides. Bake on center rack in 375°F (190°C) oven for 8 to 10 minutes. Cool for 10 minutes. Cut each meatball in half.

Spread sauce over crust. Place meatball halves over sauce, cut side down.

(continued on next page)

Sprinkle cheese over top. Grease sheet of foil and lay over top of pizza. Bake on bottom rack in 350°F (175°C) oven for 20 minutes. Remove foil. Bake for about 10 minutes. Cuts into 8 wedges.

1 wedge: 257 Calories; 9.6 g Total Fat; 317 mg Sodium; 16 g Protein; 26 g Carbohydrate; 1 g Dietary Fiber

Pictured on page 71.

CREAMY BEEF PIZZA

It's all in the name—very beefy, creamy and cheesy. Green onion adds a lot of flavor.

Pizza crust dough, your choice, pages 115 to 130 (or partially baked commercial)	1	1
Lean ground beef	³⁄₄ lb.	340 g
Tomato sauce	¹⁄₂ × 7¹⁄₂ oz.	¹⁄₂ × 213 mL
Light cream cheese, cut up	4 oz.	125 g
Dry cottage cheese	¹⁄₂ cup	125 mL
All-purpose flour	1 tbsp.	15 mL
Salt	¹⁄₂ tsp.	2 mL
Pepper	¹⁄₈ tsp.	0.5 mL
Chopped green onion	3-4 tbsp.	50-60 mL
Grated part-skim mozzarella cheese	³⁄₄ cup	175 mL
Grated part-skim mozzarella cheese	³⁄₄ cup	175 mL

Prepare pizza dough. Roll out and press in greased 12 inch (30 cm) pizza pan, forming rim around edge.

Scramble-fry ground beef in medium non-stick frying pan until no longer pink. Drain.

Beat next 6 ingredients together in medium bowl. Add beef. Add green onion. Stir together.

Sprinkle first amount of mozzarella cheese over crust. Spoon beef mixture over cheese. Sprinkle with second amount of mozzarella cheese. Bake on bottom rack in 425°F (220°C) oven for about 15 minutes, or for 8 to 10 minutes if using partially baked crust. Cuts into 8 wedges.

1 wedge: 357 Calories; 16.4 g Total Fat; 766 mg Sodium; 22 g Protein; 29 g Carbohydrate; 1 g Dietary Fiber

TACO PIZZA

Serve with green pepper strips and sour cream. The leftover beans can be frozen, or make two pizzas.

Pizza crust dough, your choice, pages 115 to 130 (or partially baked commercial)	1	1
Lean ground beef	½ lb.	225 g
Chopped onion	⅓ cup	75 mL
Canned refried beans	½ x 14 oz.	½ x 398 mL
Envelope taco seasoning mix	½ x 1¼ oz.	½ x 35 g
Tomato sauce	½ cup	125 mL
Cayenne pepper	⅛ tsp.	0.5 mL
Granulated sugar	½ tsp.	2 mL
Grated Cheddar cheese	1½ cups	375 mL

Prepare pizza dough. Roll out and press in greased 12 inch (30 cm) pizza pan, forming rim around edge.

Scramble-fry ground beef and onion in medium non-stick frying pan. Drain.

Mix next 5 ingredients in small bowl. Spread over crust. Spoon beef mixture over top.

Cover with cheese. Bake on bottom rack in 425°F (220°C) oven for about 15 minutes, or for 10 minutes if using partially baked crust. Cuts into 8 wedges.

1 wedge: 328 Calories; 14.1 g Total Fat; 697 mg Sodium; 16 g Protein; 34 g Carbohydrate; 3 g Dietary Fiber

BEEF AND MUSHROOM PIZZA

Pass the grated Parmesan cheese for this moist pizza.

Pizza crust dough, your choice, pages 115 to 130 (or partially baked commercial)	1	1
Lean ground beef	¾ lb.	340 g
Basic Pizza Sauce, page 132 (or other)	½ cup	125 mL
Grated part-skim mozzarella cheese	¾ cup	175 mL
Sliced fresh mushrooms	1¾ cups	425 mL
Grated part-skim mozzarella cheese	¾ cup	175 mL
Paprika, sprinkle		

(continued on next page)

Prepare pizza dough. Roll out and press in greased 12 inch (30 cm) pizza pan, forming rim around edge.

Scramble-fry ground beef in medium non-stick frying pan. Drain.

Spread sauce over crust. Distribute beef over sauce. Sprinkle with first amount of cheese.

Cover pizza with mushrooms. Sprinkle second amount of cheese over all. Sprinkle with paprika. Bake on bottom rack in 425°F (220°C) oven for about 15 minutes, or for about 10 minutes if using partially baked crust. Cuts into 8 wedges.

1 wedge: 288 Calories; 11.3 g Total Fat; 289 mg Sodium; 17 g Protein; 28 g Carbohydrate; 2 g Dietary Fiber

REUBEN PIZZA

If you like Reuben sandwiches, this is for you. You might choose to use the whole jar of sauerkraut.

Rye Pizza Crust dough, page 124	1	1
THOUSAND ISLAND SAUCE		
Salad dressing (or mayonnaise)	⅓ cup	75 mL
Chili sauce	3 tbsp.	50 mL
Sweet pickle relish	1½ tbsp.	25 mL
Minced onion flakes	1 tsp.	5 mL
TOPPING		
Grated Edam (or mozzarella) cheese	¾ cup	175 mL
Jar sauerkraut, drained and squeezed dry	½ × 17½ oz.	½ × 500 mL
Canned corned beef, sliced and chopped	7 oz.	200 g
Grated part-skim mozzarella cheese	¾ cup	175 mL

Prepare pizza dough. Roll out and press in greased 12 inch (30 cm) pizza pan, forming rim around edge.

Thousand Island Sauce: Mix all 4 ingredients in small bowl. Spread over crust.

Topping: Sprinkle Edam cheese over sauce. Add layer of sauerkraut. Scatter corned beef and mozzarella cheese over top. Bake on bottom rack in 425°F (220°C) oven for 13 to 15 minutes. Cuts into 8 wedges.

1 wedge: 355 Calories; 17.6 g Total Fat; 807 mg Sodium; 16 g Protein; 33 g Carbohydrate; 4 g Dietary Fiber

ORIENTAL NOODLE PIZZA

The flavorful sauce clings nicely to pepper strips and meat. Great topping for the noodles underneath.

Pizza crust dough, your choice, pages 115 to 130 (or partially baked commercial)	1	1
Package instant noodle soup with beef-flavored packet (reserve packet)	3 oz.	85 g
Boiling water, to cover		
Soy sauce	¼ cup	60 mL
Ground ginger	¼ tsp.	1 mL
Garlic powder	¼ tsp.	1 mL
Granulated sugar	1 tsp.	5 mL
Cornstarch	2 tsp.	10 mL
Reserved beef-flavored packet		
Green pepper strips	½ cup	125 mL
Red pepper strips	½ cup	125 mL
Cooking oil	2 tsp.	10 mL
Beef tenderloin (or sirloin steak), cut into thin strips	6 oz.	170 g
Basic Pizza Sauce, page 132 (or other)	½ cup	125 mL
Grated part-skim mozzarella cheese	1½ cups	375 mL

Prepare pizza dough. Roll out and press in greased 12 inch (30 cm) pizza pan, forming rim around edge.

Place noodles in medium bowl. Cover with boiling water. Let stand for 3 minutes to soften. Drain.

Combine next 6 ingredients in small saucepan. Whisk until cornstarch is dissolved. Heat and stir until boiling and thickened. Remove from heat.

Sauté green and red pepper strips in cooking oil in medium frying pan for 1 to 2 minutes. Add to soy sauce mixture.

Add beef strips to frying pan. Stir-fry for about 1 minute until half cooked. It will finish cooking in oven.

(continued on next page)

Spread sauce over crust. Layer noodles over sauce keeping in from edge. Top noodles with cheese. Try to cover noodles around edge to help keep from getting too crisp while cooking. Spoon beef mixture, including any soy sauce mixture in bowl, onto noodles. Bake on bottom rack in 425°F (220°C) oven for about 15 minutes, or for 8 to 10 minutes if using partially baked crust. Cuts into 8 wedges.

1 wedge: *317 Calories; 10.5 g Total Fat; 902 mg Sodium; 16 g Protein; 39 g Carbohydrate; 2 g Dietary Fiber*

HOLIDAY PIZZA

With a lot of extras to add color, texture and flavor.

Pizza crust dough, your choice, pages 115 to 130 (or partially baked commercial)	1	1
Lean ground beef	¾ lb.	340 g
Ground oregano	¼ tsp.	1 mL
Dried sweet basil	¼ tsp.	1 mL
Ground rosemary	¼ tsp.	1 mL
Ground thyme	¼ tsp.	1 mL
Fennel seed, crushed	¼ tsp.	1 mL
Onion powder	⅛ tsp.	0.5 mL
Garlic powder	⅛ tsp.	0.5 mL
Cayenne pepper	⅛ tsp.	0.5 mL
Basic Pizza Sauce, page 132 (or other)	⅔ cup	150 mL
Green pepper, thinly sliced into rings	1	1
Chopped green onion	2 tbsp.	30 mL
Grated part-skim mozzarella cheese	¾ cup	175 mL
Grated Parmesan cheese	¼ cup	60 mL

Prepare pizza dough. Roll out and press in greased 12 inch (30 cm) pizza pan, forming rim around edge.

Scramble-fry ground beef in medium non-stick frying pan until no longer pink. Drain.

Add next 8 ingredients. Stir together.

Spread crust with sauce. Spoon beef mixture over sauce. Spread. Arrange green pepper rings over beef. Sprinkle green onion, mozzarella cheese and Parmesan cheese over top. Bake on bottom rack in 425°F (220°C) oven for 15 to 20 minutes, or for about 8 minutes if using partially baked crust. Cuts into 8 wedges.

1 wedge: *222 Calories; 12.9 g Total Fat; 307 mg Sodium; 15 g Protein; 29 g Carbohydrate; 2 g Dietary Fiber*

SLOPPY JOE PIZZA

Sort of a make-ahead pizza. The meat topping can be ready in the refrigerator. Good with or without corn.

Frozen bread loaf dough, thawed (or other crust)	1	1
Lean ground beef	¾ lb.	340 g
All-purpose flour	¼ cup	60 mL
Condensed French onion soup	10 oz.	284 mL
Ketchup (optional)	⅓ cup	75 mL
Grated part-skim mozzarella cheese	¾ cup	175 mL
Canned (or frozen) kernel corn (optional)	⅓ cup	75 mL
Grated part-skim mozzarella cheese	¾ cup	175 mL

Roll out and stretch bread dough to fit in greased 12 inch (30 cm) pizza pan, forming rim around edge.

Scramble-fry ground beef in medium non-stick frying pan until no longer pink. Drain.

Mix in flour. Stir in soup until boiling and thickened.

Spread ketchup over crust. Layer first amount of cheese, beef mixture, corn and second amount of cheese. Bake on bottom rack in 425°F (220°C) oven for 13 to 15 minutes, or for 8 minutes if using partially baked crust. Cuts into 8 wedges.

1 wedge: *308 Calories; 10.7 g Total Fat; 704 mg Sodium; 19 g Protein; 33 g Carbohydrate; 1 g Dietary Fiber*

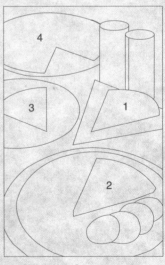

1. Western Pizza, page 43
   (on Biscuit Pizza Crust)
2. Ham And Eggs Pizza, page 45
3. Breakfast Pizza, page 41
   (on Basic Pizza Crust)
4. Sausage Hash Pizza, page 44
   (on Focaccia Pizza Crust)

Props Courtesy Of: Le Gnome
The Basket House

Topping can be ready ahead of time for a last minute snack in a hurry.

French bread loaf	1	1
Lean ground beef	1 lb.	454 g
Tomato sauce	7½ oz.	213 mL
Ground oregano	½ tsp.	2 mL
Dried sweet basil	½ tsp.	2 mL
Beef bouillon powder	½ tsp.	2 mL
Salt	¼ tsp.	1 mL
Pepper	¼ tsp.	1 mL
Onion powder	¼ tsp.	1 mL
Green onions, chopped	2	2
Sweet pickle relish	2 tbsp.	30 mL
Granulated sugar	½ tsp.	2 mL
Grated medium Cheddar cheese	1 cup	250 mL
Medium tomatoes, thinly sliced	2	2
Grated part-skim mozzarella cheese	1 cup	250 mL
Grated Parmesan cheese	2 tbsp.	30 mL

Slice loaf lengthwise into 2 halves. Arrange on ungreased baking sheet.

Scramble-fry ground beef in large non-stick frying pan until no longer pink. Drain well.

Add next 10 ingredients to beef. Stir. Spread over bread halves.

Sprinkle remaining 4 ingredients over beef mixture in order given. Bake on bottom rack in 350°F (175°C) oven for about 20 minutes. Cuts into 6 thick slices each, making 12 slices in total.

1 slice: 251 Calories; 9.6 g Total Fat; 568 mg Sodium; 16 g Protein; 25 g Carbohydrate; 1 g Dietary Fiber

Pictured on page 89.

TAMALE PIZZA

This is really different. Sure to please if you like tamales.

Cornmeal	2 tsp.	10 mL
Pizza crust dough, your choice, pages 115 to 130 (or partially baked commercial)	1	1
Canned cream-style corn	10 oz.	284 mL
Cornstarch	4 tsp.	20 mL
Lean ground beef	½ lb.	225 g
Chopped onion	½ cup	125 mL
Chopped green pepper	¼ cup	60 mL
Canned tomatoes, drained, diced and drained again	14 oz.	398 mL
Chili powder	1-1½ tsp.	5-7 mL
Garlic powder	¼ tsp.	1 mL
Salt	½ tsp.	2 mL
Pepper	⅛ tsp.	0.5 mL
Cornmeal	½ cup	125 mL
Baking powder	¼ tsp.	1 mL
Salt	¼ tsp.	1 mL
Boiling water	1¼ cups	300 mL
Grated Monterey Jack cheese	¾ cup	175 mL
Grated Monterey Jack Cheese	¾ cup	175 mL
Chopped pitted ripe olives	¼ cup	60 mL

Sprinkle bottom of greased 12 inch (30 cm) pizza pan with first amount of cornmeal. Prepare pizza dough. Roll out large enough to fit pan. Place over cornmeal, forming rim around edge. See Cornmeal Bottom, page 8.

Mix corn and cornstarch in small saucepan. Heat and stir until boiling and thickened. Set aside.

Scramble-fry ground beef, onion and green pepper in large non-stick frying pan until beef is no longer pink. Drain well.

Add next 5 ingredients. Mix well. Set aside.

Measure second amount of cornmeal, baking powder and second amount of salt into medium saucepan. Mix in boiling water. Heat and stir for about 5 minutes until very thick. Pour into greased 9 inch (22 cm) pie plate or other round container. Cool. Letting it stand in freezer or refrigerator will hurry the cooling. Turn out of pan. Cut into 8 wedges.

(continued on next page)

Spread corn mixture over crust. Sprinkle with first amount of cheese. Spoon beef mixture over cheese. Arrange cornmeal wedges evenly over top so that each finished wedge will have 1 cornmeal wedge over top. Sprinkle with second amount of cheese and olives. Bake on bottom rack in 425°F (220°C) oven for about 20 minutes, or for about 10 minutes if using partially baked crust. Cut into 8 wedges.

1 wedge: 371 Calories; 13.9 g Total Fat; 722 mg Sodium; 16 g Protein; 46 g Carbohydrate; 3 g Dietary Fiber

Pictured on page 143.

PIZZA ROYAL

Although there is a tomato layer, this contains no sauce. Like eating a warm sandwich.

Pizza crust dough, your choice, pages 115 to 130 (or partially baked commercial)	1	1
Lean ground beef	¾ lb.	340 g
Ground oregano	½ tsp.	2 mL
Salt	½ tsp.	2 mL
Cayenne pepper	⅛ tsp.	0.5 mL
Canned tomatoes, drained, chopped and drained again	14 oz.	398 mL
Chopped green onion	2 tbsp.	30 mL
Grated part-skim mozzarella cheese	1½ cups	375 mL
Grated Parmesan cheese	2 tbsp.	30 mL

Prepare pizza dough. Roll out and press in greased 12 inch (30 cm) pizza pan, forming rim around edge.

Scramble-fry ground beef in medium non-stick frying pan until no longer pink. Drain well or blot with paper towel.

Add oregano, salt and cayenne pepper. Stir together. Spread over crust.

Top with tomato. Sprinkle green onion, mozzarella cheese and Parmesan cheese over top. Bake on bottom rack in 425°F (220°C) oven for 12 to 15 minutes, or for 8 minutes if using partially baked crust. Cuts into 8 wedges.

1 wedge: 334 Calories; 13.9 g Total Fat; 531 mg Sodium; 22 g Protein; 29 g Carbohydrate; 2 g Dietary Fiber

HAMBURGER PIZZA

The crust cuts so nicely. Both hamburger and cheese show through the large chunks of tomato.

GARLIC BISCUIT PIZZA CRUST

All-purpose flour	2 cups	500 mL
Baking powder	4 tsp.	20 mL
Salt	1/4 tsp.	1 mL
Garlic salt	1 tsp.	5 mL
Milk	2/3 cup	150 mL
Cooking oil	2 tbsp.	30 mL

TOPPING

Lean ground beef	1 lb.	454 g
Chopped onion	1/2 cup	125 mL
Salt	1/2 tsp.	2 mL
Pepper	1/8 tsp.	0.5 mL
Ground sage	1/4 tsp.	1 mL
Grated part-skim mozzarella cheese	1 cup	250 mL
Canned tomatoes, drained and chopped into large pieces	14 oz.	398 mL
Granulated sugar	1 tsp.	5 mL
Dried sweet basil	1/2 tsp.	2 mL
Dried whole oregano	1/2 tsp.	2 mL

Garlic Biscuit Pizza Crust: Stir first 4 ingredients together in medium bowl. Add milk and cooking oil. Stir to form soft ball. Knead on lightly floured surface 8 times. Roll out and press in greased 12 inch (30 cm) pizza pan, forming rim around edge.

Topping: Scramble-fry ground beef and onion in medium non-stick frying pan until onion is soft and beef is no longer pink. Mix in salt, pepper and sage. Spread over crust.

Sprinkle with cheese. Arrange tomato over cheese.

Measure sugar, basil and oregano into small cup. Stir together. Sprinkle over tomato. Bake on bottom rack in 425°F (220°C) oven for 15 to 20 minutes. Cuts into 8 wedges.

1 wedge: 344 Calories; 15.2 g Total Fat; 663 mg Sodium; 19 g Protein; 32 g Carbohydrate; 2 g Dietary Fiber

Pictured on page 143.

A ring of bacon encircles egg slices. Topped with a creamy sauce.

Basic Pizza Crust dough, page 115 (or other)	1	1
All-purpose flour	3 tbsp.	50 mL
Paprika	¼ tsp.	1 mL
Salt, generous measure	¼ tsp.	1 mL
Pepper	⅛ tsp.	0.5 mL
Milk	1 cup	250 mL
Grated Monterey Jack cheese	1½ cups	375 mL
White (or alcohol-free white) wine (optional)	4 tsp.	20 mL
Picante Salsa, page 135 (or other)	⅓ cup	75 mL
Bacon slices, cut into ½ inch (12 mm) pieces	12	12
Hard-boiled eggs, thinly sliced	6	6
Paprika, sprinkle		

Prepare pizza dough. Roll out and press in greased 12 inch (30 cm) pizza pan, forming rim around edge. Poke all over with fork. If using biscuit crust, no need to poke holes. Bake on bottom rack in 425°F (220°C) oven for 5 minutes. Press down any bulges with tea towel. Continue to bake for 5 minutes until fully cooked. If starting with partially baked crust, bake for only 5 minutes.

Mix next 4 ingredients in medium saucepan. Gradually whisk in milk until no lumps remain. Heat and stir until boiling and thickened.

Add cheese and wine. Stir until cheese is melted. Remove from heat.

Spread salsa over crust.

Cook bacon in medium frying pan. Drain well. Arrange bacon around outer edge of crust. Layer egg slices in center, overlapping as you go. Spoon cheese sauce over eggs.

Sprinkle with paprika. Bake on center rack in 400°F (205°C) oven for about 10 minutes to heat through. Cuts into 8 wedges.

1 wedge: 381 Calories; 19.7 g Total Fat; 567 mg Sodium; 18 g Protein; 32 g Carbohydrate; 2 g Dietary Fiber

Pictured on page 35.

HAM PUFF PIZZA

Similar to, but better than, a ham and tomato sandwich. A whole wheat crust goes well with this also.

Basic Pizza Crust dough, page 115 (or other)	1	1
Cooking oil	1 tsp.	5 mL
Canned flakes of ham, with liquid	2 x 6½ oz	2 x 184 g
Finely chopped celery	⅔ cup	150 mL
Onion powder	¼ tsp.	1 mL
Seasoning salt	¼ tsp.	1 mL
Light salad dressing (or mayonnaise)	⅓ cup	75 mL
Tomato slices	15	15
Light salad dressing (or mayonnaise)	1¼ cups	300 mL
Grated medium Cheddar cheese	¾ cup	175 mL

Prepare pizza dough. Roll out and press in greased 12 inch (30 cm) pizza pan, forming rim around edge. Poke holes all over with fork. If using biscuit crust, no need to poke holes. Bake on bottom rack in 425°F (220°C) oven for about 10 minutes. Press down any bulges with tea towel.

Brush crust with cooking oil.

Mix next 5 ingredients in medium bowl. Spread over crust.

Arrange tomato slices over top.

Stir second amount of salad dressing and cheese together in small bowl. Spread over tomato. Broil 6 inches (15 cm) from heat for 3 to 4 minutes until pizza puffs and starts to brown lightly. Watch carefully. Cuts into 8 wedges.

1 wedge: 462 Calories; 29.4 g Total Fat; 1222 mg Sodium; 14 g Protein; 35 g Carbohydrate; 2 g Dietary Fiber

A frog's favorite television shows are the croak and dagger kind.

Like a Denver omelet on a biscuit. Good choice.

Biscuit Pizza Crust dough, page 128
    (or Biscuit Mix Pizza Crust dough,
    page 129)
	1	1

Cooking oil	1 tsp.	5 mL
Finely chopped green pepper	¼ cup	60 mL
Finely chopped onion	¼ cup	60 mL
Ketchup Pizza Sauce, page 134	⅓ cup	75 mL
Chopped cooked ham	½ cup	125 mL
Large eggs	4	4
Water	2 tbsp.	30 mL
Salt, sprinkle		
Pepper, sprinkle		

Prepare pizza dough. Roll out and press in greased 12 inch (30 cm) pizza pan, forming rim around edge.

Heat cooking oil in small frying pan. Add green pepper and onion. Sauté until soft.

Spread sauce over crust up to rim.

Mix ham and green pepper mixture in small bowl. Sprinkle over top of sauce.

Beat eggs, water, salt and pepper together in medium bowl. Pour over all. Bake on bottom rack in 375°F (190°C) oven for about 20 minutes. Cuts into 8 wedges.

1 wedge: 227 Calories; 7.9 g Total Fat; 355 mg Sodium; 9 g Protein; 30 g Carbohydrate; 2 g Dietary Fiber

Pictured on page 35.

Paré Pointer

Did you know that one dinosaur went on a diet. He began by eating a cottage cheese factory.

SAUSAGE HASH PIZZA

Sausage and potato on toasty bread. A good breakfast.

Focaccia Pizza Crust, page 120	1	1
Small link sausages (½ lb., 225 g), cut into ¼ inch (6 mm) coins	8	8
Chopped onion	½ cup	125 mL
Frozen hash brown potatoes, thawed	2 cups	500 mL
Salt	½-1 tsp.	2-5 mL
Pepper	¼-½ tsp.	1-2 mL
Grated Edam (or mozzarella) cheese	¾ cup	175 mL
Grated part-skim mozzarella cheese	¾ cup	175 mL
Herbed spreadable cream cheese	½ cup	125 mL

Prepare crust as directed in recipe.

Stir-fry sausage and onion in medium frying pan until onion is soft and sausage is no longer pink. Drain well.

Place hash browns in medium bowl. Sprinkle with salt and pepper.

Toss both cheeses together in small bowl.

Spread cream cheese evenly on crust. Add layers of sausage mixture, hash browns and cheese. Bake on bottom rack in 400°F (205°C) oven for about 10 minutes. Cuts into 8 wedges.

1 wedge: 378 Calories; 19.2 g Total Fat; 580 mg Sodium; 14 g Protein; 38 g Carbohydrate; 2 g Dietary Fiber

Variation: Omit herbed cream cheese. Spread crust with ¼ cup (60 mL) jalapeño jelly.

Pictured on page 35.

Some bees are so quiet they are known as mumble bees.

Tomato sauce is good in this but be sure to try it with jalapeño jelly. A full meal.

Pizza crust dough, your choice, pages 115 to 130 (or partially baked commercial)	1	1
Hard margarine (or butter)	1 tbsp.	15 mL
Large eggs	12	12
Water	⅓ cup	75 mL
Salt	1 tsp.	5 mL
Pepper	¼ tsp.	1 mL
Favorite Tomato Pizza Sauce, page 138 (or jalapeño jelly)	½ cup	125 mL
Cooked ham (at least ⅛ inch, 3 mm thick), cut into ½ × 1 inch (12 mm × 2.5 cm) pieces	10 oz.	285 g
Grated Edam cheese	¾ cup	175 mL
Grated part-skim mozzarella cheese	¾ cup	175 mL

Prepare pizza dough. Roll out and press in greased 12 inch (30 cm) pizza pan, forming rim around edge.

Melt margarine in large non-stick frying pan. Beat next 4 ingredients together in medium bowl. Pour into frying pan. Scramble-fry until egg is cooked. Do not overcook.

Spread crust with sauce. Spoon eggs over top.

Top with ham. Toss both cheeses together in small bowl. Layer over ham. Bake on bottom rack in 425°F (220°C) oven for 13 to 15 minutes, or for about 8 minutes if using partially baked crust. Cuts into 8 wedges.

1 wedge: 397 Calories; 20.1 g Total Fat; 1092 mg Sodium; 23 g Protein; 30 g Carbohydrate; 1 g Dietary Fiber

Pictured on page 35.

Paré Pointer

A sick sailor can't go to sea and a blind sailor can't see to go.

SEAFOOD CALZONES

Pronounced kal-ZOH-nay. This extra special dish contains shrimp, crab and scallops.

Basic Pizza Crust dough, page 115	1	1
Hard margarine (or butter)	2 tbsp.	30 mL
All-purpose flour	2 tbsp.	30 mL
Dry mustard, just a pinch		
Salt, sprinkle		
Pepper, sprinkle		
Milk	½ cup	125 mL
Non-fat sour cream	¼ cup	60 mL
Sherry (or alcohol-free sherry)	1-2 tbsp.	15-30 mL
Cooked small fresh (or canned) shrimp	¼ lb.	113 g
Fresh crabmeat (or 1 can, 4 oz., 113 g, drained and cartilage removed)	¼ lb.	113 g
Fresh (or frozen) scallops	3 oz.	85 g
Boiling water		
Seafood Cocktail Sauce, page 12 (or commercial)	¼ cup	60 mL
Grated part-skim mozzarella cheese	1⅓ cups	325 mL

Prepare pizza dough. Divide into 4 equal balls. Cover. Let rest while preparing filling.

Melt margarine in medium saucepan. Mix in flour, dry mustard, salt and pepper. Stir in milk. Heat and stir together until mixture is boiling and thickened. Mixture will be quite thick.

Stir in sour cream and sherry.

Add shrimp and crabmeat. Stir together. Set aside.

Cook scallops in boiling water for 3 to 5 minutes, depending on size, until they lose their translucent appearance. Drain. If scallops are large, cut into size of miniature marshmallows. Add scallops to sauce. Stir together.

Roll out 1 ball of dough on lightly floured surface into ⅛ inch (3 mm) thick circle. Spread ½ of circle with 1 tbsp. (15 mL) cocktail sauce, keeping in from edge about 1 inch (2.5 cm). Spread ¼ of seafood mixture over cocktail sauce. Sprinkle with ⅓ cup (75 mL) cheese. Dampen edge with water. Fold over and press to seal, folding edge upward and over. Crimp edge with fork. Repeat, making 3 more. Place on greased baking sheet. Poke holes in top. Bake on bottom rack in 425°F (220°C) oven for about 15 minutes. Makes 4 calzones.

1 calzone: 579 Calories; 21.1 g Total Fat; 923 mg Sodium; 31 g Protein; 63 g Carbohydrate; 2 g Dietary Fiber

Pictured on page 125.

SWEET AND SOUR CALZONES

No tomato sauce or cheese in this. Just a pure delicious sweet and sour taste.

Basic Pizza Crust dough, page 115	1	1
Cooking oil	1 tbsp.	15 mL
Pork tenderloin, cut into thin strips	¾ lb.	340 g
Onion slivers	½ cup	125 mL
Green pepper slivers	½ cup	125 mL
White vinegar	¼ cup	60 mL
Brown sugar, packed	¼ cup	60 mL
Soy sauce	1 tbsp.	15 mL
Canned pineapple tidbits, with juice	8 oz.	227 mL
Cornstarch	2 tbsp.	30 mL

Prepare pizza dough. Divide into 4 equal balls. Cover. Let rest while preparing filling.

Heat cooking oil in medium frying pan. Add pork strips, onion and green pepper. Stir-fry for 1 to 2 minutes until pork is no longer pink. Remove from heat.

Combine remaining 5 ingredients in small saucepan. Stir until cornstarch is dissolved. Heat and stir until boiling and thickened. Remove from heat. Add pork mixture. Stir together. Cool slightly.

Roll out 1 ball of dough on lightly floured surface into ⅛ inch (3 mm) thick circle. Spread ½ of circle with ¼ of sweet and sour mixture, keeping in from edge about 1 inch (2.5 cm). Dampen edge with water. Fold over and press to seal, folding edge upward and over. Crimp edge with fork. Repeat, making 3 more. Place on greased baking sheet. Poke holes in top. Bake on bottom rack in 425°F (220°C) oven for about 15 minutes. Makes 4 calzones.

1 calzone: 554 Calories; 13.3 g Total Fat; 481 mg Sodium; 26 g Protein; 82 g Carbohydrate; 4 g Dietary Fiber

A tiger looks like a lion in jail.

HAM AND CHEESE CALZONES

Very colorful filling.

Whole Wheat Pizza Crust dough, page 117 (or Basic Pizza Crust dough, page 115)	1	1
Cooking oil	2 tsp.	10 mL
Chopped green pepper	½ cup	125 mL
Chopped red pepper	½ cup	125 mL
Canned sliced mushrooms, drained	10 oz.	284 mL
Garlic powder	¼ tsp.	1 mL
Salt	¼ tsp.	1 mL
Pepper	¹⁄₁₆ tsp.	0.5 mL
Basic Pizza Sauce, page 132 (or other)	¼ cup	60 mL
Canned flakes of ham, drained and crumbled	6½ oz.	184 g
Grated Parmesan cheese	4 tsp.	20 mL
Grated Muenster cheese	1 cup	250 mL

Prepare pizza dough. Divide dough into 4 equal balls. Cover. Let rest while preparing filling.

Heat cooking oil in medium frying pan. Add green and red pepper. Sauté until tender-crisp. Remove from heat.

Add mushrooms, garlic powder, salt and pepper. Stir together.

Roll out 1 ball of dough on lightly floured surface into ⅛ inch (3 mm) thick circle. Spread ½ of circle with 1 tbsp. (15 mL) sauce, keeping in from edge about 1 inch (2.5 cm). Spoon ¼ of mushroom mixture over top. Add layer of ¼ of ham over top. Sprinkle with 1 tsp. (5 mL) Parmesan cheese and ¼ cup (60 mL) Muenster cheese. Dampen edge with water. Fold over and press to seal, folding edge upward and over. Crimp edge with fork. Repeat, making 3 more. Place on greased baking sheet. Poke holes in top. Bake on bottom rack in 425°F (220°C) oven for about 15 minutes. Makes 4 calzones.

1 calzone: 569 Calories; 28.8 g Total Fat; 1425 mg Sodium; 25 g Protein; 55 g Carbohydrate; 7 g Dietary Fiber

Pictured on page 89.

This could easily be one of your favorites. It's incredibly good.

Basic Pizza Crust dough, page 115	1	1
Beef stew meat, cut into ½ inch (12 mm) cubes (or smaller)	¾ lb.	340 g
Cooking oil	2 tsp.	10 mL
Water, to cover		
Salt	½ tsp.	2 mL
Pepper	⅛ tsp.	0.5 mL
Chopped onion	½ cup	125 mL
Basic Pizza Sauce, page 132	¼ cup	60 mL
Canned asparagus tips, drained	12 oz.	341 mL
Grated part-skim mozzarella cheese	1⅓ cups	325 mL

Prepare pizza dough. Divide into 4 equal balls. Cover. Let rest while preparing filling.

Brown beef in hot cooking oil in medium frying pan. Spoon into large saucepan.

Pour about 1 cup (250 mL) water into frying pan. Loosen all browned bits. Pour over beef in saucepan. Add water to cover, salt and pepper. Boil gently for 1 hour.

Add onion. Boil for 30 minutes. Strain, saving broth for soup if you like. Spread beef on large plate to cool.

Roll out 1 ball of dough on lightly floured surface into ⅛ inch (3 mm) thick circle. Spread ¼ of sauce over ½ of circle, keeping in from edge about 1 inch (2.5 cm). Layer ¼ of beef mixture over sauce. Lay about 5 asparagus tips side by side over top. Sprinkle with ⅓ cup (75 mL) cheese. Dampen edge with water. Fold over and press to seal, folding edge upward and over. Crimp edge with fork. Repeat, making 3 more. Place on greased baking sheet. Poke holes in top. Bake on bottom rack in 425°F (220°C) oven for about 15 minutes. Makes 4 calzones.

1 calzone: 596 Calories; 23.2 g Total Fat; 1165 mg Sodium; 38 g Protein; 58 g Carbohydrate; 4 g Dietary Fiber

RIB CALZONES

A surprise flavor booster. A touch of mincemeat adds spice to this meaty filling.

Basic Pizza Crust dough, page 115	1	1
Pork spareribs, cut into 3 rib sections	1¼ lbs.	568 g
Salt	¾ tsp.	4 mL
Water, to cover		
Mincemeat pie filling	¼ cup	60 mL
Grated part-skim mozzarella cheese	1⅓ cups	325 mL

Prepare pizza dough. Divide into 4 equal balls. Cover. Let rest while preparing filling.

Combine spareribs, salt and water in large saucepan. Bring to a boil. Boil slowly for about 1½ hours until ribs are tender. Drain. Remove bones. Cut pork into bite-size pieces.

Roll out 1 ball of dough on lightly floured surface into ⅛ inch (3 mm) thick circle. Spread scant 1 tbsp. (15 mL) mincemeat over ½ of circle, keeping in from edge about 1 inch (2.5 cm). Place ¼ of pork over top. Sprinkle with ⅓ cup (75 mL) cheese. Dampen edge with water. Fold over and press to seal, folding edge upward and over. Crimp edge with fork. Repeat, making 3 more. Place on greased baking sheet. Poke holes in top. Bake on bottom rack in 425°F (220°C) oven for about 15 minutes. Makes 4 calzones.

1 calzone: 888 Calories; 52.6 g Total Fat; 1012 mg Sodium; 41 g Protein; 60 g Carbohydrate; 2 g Dietary Fiber

A cricket is an English grasshopper.

CHICKEN HOT-HOT PIZZA

Great taste as is. And you can add more curry powder and cayenne pepper if you like.

Pizza crust dough, your choice, pages 115 to 130 (or partially baked commercial)	1	1
CURRY SAUCE		
Chopped onion	¼ cup	60 mL
Cooking oil	2 tsp.	10 mL
All-purpose flour	2 tsp.	10 mL
Curry powder	2 tsp.	10 mL
Cayenne pepper	⅛ tsp.	0.5 mL
Ketchup	½ tsp.	2 mL
Lemon juice	¼ tsp.	1 mL
Granulated sugar	½ tsp.	2 mL
Salt	¼ tsp.	1 mL
Pepper, just a pinch		
Red (or alcohol-free red) wine	⅓ cup	75 mL
Apricot jam	1 tbsp.	15 mL
Light salad dressing (or mayonnaise)	⅓ cup	75 mL
Boneless, skinless chicken breast halves (about 3)	¾ lb.	340 g
Small red onion, slivered	1	1
Medium carrot, cut julienne	1	1
Cooking oil	2 tsp.	10 mL
Grated part-skim mozzarella cheese	1 cup	250 mL

Prepare pizza dough. Roll out and press in greased 12 inch (30 cm) pizza pan, forming rim around edge.

Curry Sauce: Sauté onion in cooking oil in small saucepan until soft. Mix in next 9 ingredients. Heat and stir together until sauce is boiling and thickened.

Stir in jam and salad dressing.

Sauté chicken, red onion and carrot in cooking oil in medium frying pan until chicken is barely cooked. Cut chicken into ¼ x 1 inch (6 mm x 2.5 cm) pieces.

Sprinkle cheese over crust. Spoon chicken mixture over cheese. Drizzle sauce over top, spreading to edge. Bake on bottom rack in 425°F (220°C) oven for about 15 minutes, or for about 10 minutes if using partially baked crust. Cuts into 8 wedges.

1 wedge: 292 Calories; 9.6 g Total Fat; 290 mg Sodium; 18 g Protein; 31 g Carbohydrate; 2 g Dietary Fiber

BARBECUED CHICKEN PIZZA

A bit of a barbecue flavor from the sauce adds to this flavorful pizza.

Pizza crust dough, your choice, pages 115 to 130 (or partially baked commercial)	1	1
Cooking oil	2 tsp.	10 mL
Boneless, skinless chicken breast halves (about 3), cut bite size	¾ lb.	340 g
Chopped onion	½ cup	125 mL
Smoky sweet barbecue sauce	½ cup	125 mL
Grated Monterey Jack cheese	¾ cup	175 mL
Grated mozzarella cheese	¾ cup	175 mL

Prepare pizza dough. Roll out and press in greased 12 inch (30 cm) pizza pan, forming rim around edge.

Combine cooking oil, chicken and onion in medium frying pan. Sauté until chicken is not quite cooked.

Stir in barbecue sauce. Cook for 2 to 3 minutes. Remove from heat to cool slightly.

Sprinkle crust with Monterey Jack cheese. Spoon chicken mixture over top. Sprinkle with mozzarella cheese. Bake on bottom rack in 425°F (220°C) oven for about 15 minutes, or for 8 to 10 minutes if using partially baked crust. Cuts into 8 wedges.

1 wedge: *297 Calories; 11 g Total Fat; 362 mg Sodium; 19 g Protein; 29 g Carbohydrate; 2 g Dietary Fiber*

Pictured on page 89.

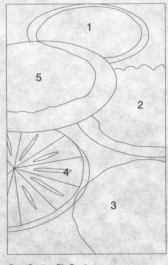

1. Choco Vanilla Pizza, page 77
2. Pizza Flan, page 84
3. Cookie Pizza, page 83
4. Red Spoke Pizza, page 86
5. Cherry Cheese Pizza, page 74

Props Courtesy Of: Dansk
The Doulton Store

Chicken Pizzas

This will be a big hit. The smoky cheese flavor is a nice change from mozzarella.

Pizza crust dough, your choice, pages 115 to 130 (or partially baked commercial)	1	1
Cooking oil	2 tsp.	10 mL
Boneless, skinless chicken breast halves (about 3), cut bite size	¾ lb.	340 g
Cooking oil	1 tsp.	5 mL
Medium red onion, cut lengthwise in half, sliced paper-thin	1	1
Basic Pizza Sauce, page 132	½ cup	125 mL
Grated smoked provolone cheese	¾ cup	175 mL
Grated smoked provolone cheese	¾ cup	175 mL
Grated fontina cheese	½ cup	125 mL

Prepare pizza dough. Roll out and press in greased 12 inch (30 cm) pizza pan, forming rim around edge.

Heat first amount of cooking oil in medium frying pan. Add chicken. Sauté until barely cooked. Remove to medium bowl.

Add second amount of cooking oil to frying pan. Add red onion. Sauté until soft. Cool slightly.

Spread sauce over crust. Sprinkle first amount of provolone cheese, chicken and onion over sauce. Sprinkle second amount of provolone cheese and fontina cheese over top. Bake on bottom rack in 425°F (220°C) oven for about 13 minutes, or for about 8 minutes if using partially baked crust. Cuts into 8 wedges.

1 wedge: 334 Calories; 14.5 g Total Fat; 442 mg Sodium; 21 g Protein; 29 g Carbohydrate; 2 g Dietary Fiber

Baby robot to his mother "I love you watts and watts."

THAI GOODNESS PIZZA

Scrumptious is the word for this. Has just the right heat.

Pizza crust dough, your choice, pages 115 to 130 (or partially baked commercial)	1	1
PEANUT SAUCE		
Smooth peanut butter	¼ cup	60 mL
Reserved pineapple juice	3 tbsp.	50 mL
Soy sauce	1 tbsp.	15 mL
Lemon juice	2 tsp.	10 mL
Cooking oil	2 tsp.	10 mL
Liquid honey	1 tsp.	5 mL
Minced fresh gingerroot	1 tsp.	5 mL
Garlic powder	½ tsp.	2 mL
Onion powder	¼ tsp.	1 mL
Cayenne pepper	¼ tsp.	1 mL
Cooking oil	1 tbsp.	15 mL
Red pepper, slivered	1	1
Small red onion, slivered	1	1
Boneless, skinless chicken breast halves (about 2), diced	½ lb.	225 g
Grated part-skim mozzarella cheese	½ cup	125 mL
Frozen pea pods, thawed and blotted dry (or 5 oz., 140 g, fresh, blanched)	½ × 10 oz.	½ × 284 g
Pineapple tidbits, drained, juice reserved	½ cup	125 mL
Grated part-skim mozzarella cheese	¾ cup	175 mL

Prepare pizza dough. Roll out and press in greased 12 inch (30 cm) pizza pan, forming rim around edge.

Peanut Sauce: Combine all 10 ingredients in small saucepan. Heat and stir together until smooth and almost boiling. Remove from heat.

Heat cooking oil in medium frying pan. Add red pepper, red onion and chicken. Sauté until onion is soft and chicken is barely cooked.

Spread peanut sauce over crust. Sprinkle with first amount of cheese. Spoon chicken mixture over cheese. Scatter pea pods and pineapple over chicken. Sprinkle second amount of cheese over all. Bake on bottom rack in 425°F (220°C) oven for about 15 minutes, or for 8 to 10 minutes if using partially baked crust. Cuts into 8 wedges.

1 wedge: 334 Calories; 14.4 g Total Fat; 366 mg Sodium; 18 g Protein; 34 g Carbohydrate; 2 g Dietary Fiber

Pictured on front cover.

After baking, this is topped with fresh tomato for a gorgeous colorful appearance.

Frozen whole wheat bread loaf dough, thawed	1	1
Cooking oil	1 tbsp.	15 mL
Boneless, skinless chicken breast halves (about 2), cut into ¾ inch (2 cm) cubes	½ lb.	225 g
Chopped onion	½ cup	125 mL
Small green pepper, cut into slivers	1	1
Favorite Tomato Pizza Sauce, page 138 (or other)	½ cup	125 mL
Grated part-skim mozzarella cheese	¾ cup	175 mL
Canned mushroom pieces, drained	10 oz.	284 mL
Grated part-skim mozzarella cheese	¾ cup	175 mL
Grated Parmesan cheese	1 tbsp.	15 mL
Cherry tomatoes, sliced (see Note)	6-8	6-8

Roll out and press dough in greased 12 inch (30 cm) pizza pan, forming rim around edge.

Heat cooking oil in medium frying pan. Add chicken, onion and green pepper. Sauté until chicken is barely cooked.

Spread sauce over crust. Sprinkle with first amount of mozzarella cheese. Spoon chicken mixture over cheese. Scatter mushrooms over top. Sprinkle with second amount of mozzarella cheese and Parmesan cheese. Bake on bottom rack in 425°F (220°C) oven for about 15 minutes, or for about 8 minutes if using partially baked crust.

Arrange tomato slices over top. Cuts into 8 wedges.

Note: If you prefer your tomato cooked, add before or after second amount of mozzarella cheese is added.

1 wedge: 279 Calories; 7.9 g Total Fat; 652 mg Sodium; 19 g Protein; 36 g Carbohydrate; 5 g Dietary Fiber

MEXICAN PIZZA CON POLLO

A substantial topping that has a yummy Mexican flavor. Serve with a dish of sour cream on the side.

Taco Pizza Crust dough, page 115	**1**	**1**
Cooking oil	**2 tsp.**	**10 mL**
Chopped onion	**1 cup**	**250 mL**
Boneless, skinless chicken breast halves (about 2), cut into ½ inch (12 mm) pieces	**½ lb.**	**225 g**
Canned refried beans (freeze ½ can, or make 2 pizzas)	**½ × 14 oz.**	**½ × 398 mL**
Picante Salsa, page 135 (or commercial)	**⅔ cup**	**150 mL**
Canned diced green chilies, with liquid	**4 oz.**	**114 mL**
Grated medium Cheddar cheese	**1 cup**	**250 mL**
Grated Monterey Jack cheese	**½ cup**	**125 mL**

Prepare pizza dough. Roll out and press in greased 12 inch (30 cm) pizza pan, forming rim around edge.

Heat cooking oil in medium frying pan. Add onion and chicken. Sauté until onion is soft and chicken is no longer pink.

Spread refried beans over crust. Spread salsa over beans.

Stir green chilies into chicken mixture. Spread over salsa.

Sprinkle with Cheddar cheese then with Monterey Jack cheese. Bake on bottom rack in 425°F (220°C) oven for 18 to 20 minutes. Cuts into 8 wedges.

1 wedge: 341 Calories; 13 g Total Fat; 852 mg Sodium; 18 g Protein; 38 g Carbohydrate; 4 g Dietary Fiber

Be sure to pay for acupuncture with pin money.

CREAMY CHICKEN PIZZA

Colorful peppers mingle with chicken. Good choice.

Pizza crust dough, your choice, pages 115 to 130 (or partially baked commercial)	1	1
Cooking oil	2 tsp.	10 mL
Medium green pepper, chopped	½	½
Medium red pepper, chopped	½	½
Chopped fresh mushrooms	1½ cups	375 mL
Chopped onion	½ cup	125 mL
All-purpose flour	2 tbsp.	30 mL
Chicken bouillon powder	½ tsp.	2 mL
Salt	½ tsp.	2 mL
Pepper	⅛ tsp.	0.5 mL
Milk	½ cup	125 mL
Chopped cooked chicken or turkey (or 1 can, 6½ oz., 184 g, drained and broken up)	1 cup	250 mL
Grated part-skim mozzarella cheese	¾ cup	175 mL

Prepare pizza dough. Roll out and press in greased 12 inch (30 cm) pizza pan, forming rim around edge.

Heat cooking oil in large frying pan. Add green and red pepper, mushrooms and onion. Sauté until soft.

Mix flour, bouillon powder, salt and pepper in small bowl. Stir into vegetable mixture. Stir in milk until mixture is boiling and thickened.

Add chicken. Stir together. Spread over pizza crust.

Sprinkle cheese over top. Bake on bottom rack in 425°F (220°C) oven for 13 to 15 minutes, or for about 8 minutes if using partially baked crust. Cuts into 8 wedges.

1 wedge: 249 Calories; 7.8 g Total Fat; 373 mg Sodium; 14 g Protein; 31 g Carbohydrate; 2 g Dietary Fiber

CHICKEN ONION PIZZA

Try a sauce of sour cream rather than a tomato sauce. The caramelized onion is so good.

Pizza crust dough, your choice, pages 115 to 130 (or partially baked commercial)	1	1
Water	3 tbsp.	50 mL
Liquid gravy browner	1/4 tsp.	1 mL
Medium onion, sliced 1/8 inch (3 mm) thick	1	1
Hard margarine (or butter)	1 tsp.	5 mL
Hard margarine (or butter)	1 tsp.	5 mL
Boneless, skinless chicken breast halves (about 2), cut into short slivers	1/2 lb.	225 g
Sliced fresh mushrooms	2 cups	500 mL
Non-fat sour cream	1/2 cup	125 mL
Grated part-skim mozzarella cheese	1/2 cup	125 mL
Grated part-skim mozzarella cheese	1/2 cup	125 mL
Chopped or diced green pepper	1/2 cup	125 mL

Prepare pizza dough. Roll out and press in greased 12 inch (30 cm) pizza pan, forming rim around edge.

Combine water and gravy browner in small frying pan. Stir together. Add onion. Cover. Steam slowly until water is evaporated. Add first amount of margarine. Sauté until caramelized.

Heat second amount of margarine in medium non-stick frying pan. Add chicken. Sauté for about 5 minutes. Add mushrooms. Cook until liquid is evaporated.

Spread crust with sour cream. Sprinkle with first amount of cheese. Layer onion and chicken mixture over cheese. Sprinkle with second amount of cheese. Scatter green pepper over top. Bake on bottom rack in 425°F (220°C) oven for 13 to 15 minutes, or for 8 to 9 minutes if using partially baked crust. Cuts into 8 wedges.

1 wedge: 253 Calories; 7.8 g Total Fat; 201 mg Sodium; 15 g Protein; 30 g Carbohydrate; 2 g Dietary Fiber

CHICKEN MUENSTER PIZZA

Mild yet a different flavor from this good cheese.

Pizza crust dough, your choice, pages 115 to 130 (or partially baked commercial)	1	1
Cooking oil	2 tsp.	10 mL
Boneless, skinless chicken breast halves (about 2), cut into small chunks	½ lb.	225 g
Basic Pizza Sauce, page 132 (or other)	½ cup	125 mL
Grated Muenster cheese	1½ cups	375 mL
Fine dry bread crumbs	¼ cup	60 mL
Italian seasoning	¾ tsp.	4 mL

Prepare pizza dough. Roll out and press in greased 12 inch (30 cm) pizza pan, forming rim around edge.

Put cooking oil and chicken into medium frying pan. Sauté for about 5 minutes until chicken is no longer pink.

Spread sauce over crust. Scatter chicken over top.

Measure cheese, bread crumbs and Italian seasoning into small bowl. Toss together to mix well. Sprinkle over top of chicken. Bake on bottom rack in 425°F (220°C) oven for 13 to 15 minutes, or for 8 minutes if using partially baked crust. Cuts into 8 wedges.

1 wedge: 299 Calories; 12.4 g Total Fat; 394 mg Sodium; 16 g Protein; 30 g Carbohydrate; 2 g Dietary Fiber

Paré Pointer

Confucius say, "Little pig who eat big meal, make hog of himself."

CHICKEN DELUXE PIZZA

Complete with cranberries and a touch of wine.

Cooking oil	1 tbsp.	15 mL
White (or alcohol-free white) wine	¼ cup	60 mL
Ground rosemary (or thyme)	½ tsp.	2 mL
Boneless, skinless chicken breast halves (about 3), cut into scant ½ inch (12 mm) cubes	¾ lb.	340 g
Sliced fresh mushrooms	2 cups	500 mL
Chopped onion	½ cup	125 mL
Dried cranberries	⅓ cup	75 mL
Salt, sprinkle		
Pepper, sprinkle		
Frozen whole wheat bread loaf dough, thawed	1	1
Basic Pizza Sauce, page 132 (or other)	½ cup	125 mL
Grated Monterey Jack cheese	¾ cup	175 mL
Grated part-skim mozzarella cheese	¾ cup	175 mL

Heat cooking oil, wine and rosemary in large frying pan. Stir together.

Add chicken, mushrooms, onion and cranberries. Stir together. Bring to a gentle boil. Cover. Boil slowly for about 10 minutes. Remove cover. Continue to boil gently until liquid is evaporated. If chicken juices run pink, stir-fry until cooked.

Sprinkle with salt and pepper. Stir together. Remove from heat before shaping crust.

Roll out and press bread dough in greased 12 inch (30 cm) pizza pan, forming rim around edge.

Spread sauce over crust. Cover sauce with chicken mixture.

Sprinkle Monterey Jack cheese over top, followed by mozzarella cheese. Bake on bottom rack in 425°F (220°C) oven for about 10 minutes. Cuts into 8 wedges.

1 wedge: 309 Calories; 9.4 g Total Fat; 537 mg Sodium; 22 g Protein; 36 g Carbohydrate; 5 g Dietary Fiber

Lip smacking good. Bound to be a favorite.

Pizza crust dough, your choice, pages 115 to 130 (or partially baked commercial)	1	1
PEANUT HOT SAUCE		
Smooth peanut butter	½ cup	125 mL
Water	¼ cup	60 mL
White vinegar	2 tbsp.	30 mL
Brown sugar, packed	3 tbsp.	50 mL
Soy sauce	2 tbsp.	30 mL
Dried crushed chilies	1 tsp.	5 mL
Ground ginger	¼ tsp.	1 mL
Garlic powder	¼ tsp.	1 mL
Boneless, skinless chicken breast halves (about 2), cut into ½ inch (12 mm) pieces	½ lb.	225 g
Cooking oil	2 tsp.	10 mL
Grated part-skim mozzarella cheese	1½ cups	375 mL
Bean sprouts (large handful)	1 cup	250 mL
Green onions, sliced	2	2
Chopped peanuts	2 tbsp.	30 mL

Prepare pizza dough. Roll out and press in greased 12 inch (30 cm) pizza pan, forming rim around edge.

Peanut Hot Sauce: Combine all 8 ingredients in small saucepan. Simmer for 5 minutes. Sauce will be thick. Pour ½ of sauce into small bowl. Set aside.

Sauté chicken in cooking oil in medium frying pan for about 5 minutes until cooked. Add chicken to sauce in bowl. Stir together.

Spread remaining ½ of sauce over crust. Sprinkle with cheese. Spoon chicken mixture over cheese. Add layer of bean sprouts. Sprinkle with green onion and peanuts. Bake on bottom rack in 425°F (220°C) oven for 13 to 15 minutes, or for 9 minutes if using partially baked crust. Cuts into 8 wedges.

1 wedge: 394 Calories; 18.6 g Total Fat; 556 mg Sodium; 21 g Protein; 37 g Carbohydrate; 3 g Dietary Fiber

CHICKEN STROGANOFF PIZZA

Delicious and so satisfying. A hand eaten stroganoff is indeed unusual.

Pizza crust dough, your choice, pages 115 to 130 (or partially baked commercial)	1	1
Cooking oil	1 tsp.	5 mL
Boneless, skinless chicken breast halves (about 2), cut into 1/4 x 1 inch (6 mm x 2.5 cm) strips	1/2 lb.	225 g
Cooking oil	1 tsp.	5 mL
Chopped onion	1 cup	250 mL
Sliced fresh mushrooms	1 cup	250 mL
STROGANOFF SAUCE		
Finely chopped fresh mushrooms	3 tbsp.	50 mL
Hard margarine (or butter)	1 tsp.	5 mL
Water	1/2 cup	125 mL
Beef bouillon powder	1 tsp.	5 mL
Dill weed	1/4 tsp.	1 mL
Salt, sprinkle		
Pepper, sprinkle		
Paprika, sprinkle		
Water	1 tbsp.	15 mL
Cornstarch	1 tbsp.	15 mL
Sour cream	1/3 cup	75 mL
Grated part-skim mozzarella cheese	3/4 cup	175 mL

Prepare pizza dough. Roll out and press in greased 12 inch (30 cm) pizza pan, forming rim around edge.

Put first amount of cooking oil and chicken into medium frying pan. Sauté for about 5 minutes to cook. Remove to medium bowl.

Put second amount of cooking oil, onion and mushrooms into pan. Sauté until vegetables are soft. Add to chicken in bowl.

Stroganoff Sauce: Sauté mushrooms in margarine in medium frying pan until soft. Add next 6 ingredients. Stir together. Bring mixture to a boil.

(continued on next page)

Mix water and cornstarch in small cup. Stir into sauce until it returns to a boil and thickens. Add sour cream. Stir together. Add chicken mixture to sauce. Stir. Spread over crust.

Sprinkle with cheese. Bake on bottom rack in 425°F (220°C) oven for 13 to 15 minutes, or for about 8 minutes if using partially baked crust. Cuts into 8 wedges.

1 wedge: 258 Calories; 9.1 g Total Fat; 243 mg Sodium; 14 g Protein; 30 g Carbohydrate; 2 g Dietary Fiber

CURRIED CHICKEN PIZZA

A mild curry flavor which can easily be increased if desired.

Rice Pizza Crust, page 122	1	1
Cooking oil	1 tbsp.	15 mL
Boneless, skinless chicken breast halves (about 3)	¾ lb.	340 g
Chopped onion	¼ cup	60 mL
Curry powder	1 tsp.	5 mL
Salt	¼ tsp.	1 mL
All-purpose flour	3 tbsp.	50 mL
Chicken bouillon powder	1 tsp.	5 mL
Milk	1 cup	250 mL
Basic Pizza Sauce, page 132 (or other)	½ cup	125 mL
Grated part-skim mozzarella cheese	1½ cups	375 mL
Paprika, sprinkle		

Prepare crust according to recipe.

Heat cooking oil in large frying pan. Add chicken and onion. Sauté until chicken is no longer pink. Remove chicken and cut into short strips. Return to pan.

Mix in curry powder, salt, flour and bouillon powder. Stir in milk until mixture is boiling and thickened.

Spread sauce over crust. Spoon chicken mixture over sauce.

Sprinkle with cheese and paprika. Bake on bottom rack in 425°F (220°C) oven for about 15 minutes. Cuts into 8 wedges.

1 wedge: 293 Calories; 6.9 g Total Fat; 393 mg Sodium; 21 g Protein; 36 g Carbohydrate; 2 g Dietary Fiber

BLACKENED CHICKEN PIZZA

This has been known to set off smoke alarms. Pan frying on the barbecue is the answer, or at least turn the kitchen fan on high.

Basic (or Thin Basic) Pizza Crust dough, page 115 (or partially baked commercial)	1	1
Paprika	1 tbsp.	15 mL
Chili powder	1 tsp.	5 mL
Onion powder	1 tsp.	5 mL
Seasoning salt	1/2 tsp.	2 mL
Ground thyme	1/2 tsp.	2 mL
Cayenne pepper	1/2 tsp.	2 mL
Garlic powder	1/8 tsp.	0.5 mL
Salt	1/2 tsp.	2 mL
Pepper	1/2 tsp.	2 mL
Boneless, skinless chicken breast halves (about 3), pounded flat	3/4 lb.	340 g
Cooking oil	2 tsp.	10 mL
Small zucchini slices	3/4 cup	175 mL
Chopped onion	1/2 cup	125 mL
Cooking oil	1 tsp.	5 mL
Basic Pizza Sauce, page 132 (or other)	1/2 cup	125 mL
Grated part-skim mozzarella cheese	3/4 cup	175 mL
Grated part-skim mozzarella cheese	3/4 cup	175 mL
Slivered red pepper	1/2 cup	125 mL

Prepare pizza dough. Roll out and press in greased 12 inch (30 cm) pizza pan, forming rim around edge.

Measure next 9 ingredients into shallow bowl. Stir together.

Brush chicken with first amount of cooking oil. Coat with dry mixture. Heat heavy frying pan until drops of water bounce all over rather than remain in one spot and sizzle. Add chicken. It will cook quickly. When blackened on both sides, remove to cutting board. Cut into 3/4 inch (2 cm) pieces.

(continued on next page)

Sauté zucchini and onion in second amount of cooking oil in medium frying pan until soft.

Spread sauce over crust. Sprinkle with first amount of cheese. Scatter chicken over cheese. Add layers of zucchini mixture, second amount of cheese and red pepper. Bake on bottom rack in 425°F (220°C) oven for about 15 minutes, or for 8 to 10 minutes if using partially baked crust. Cuts into 8 wedges.

1 wedge: 294 Calories; 10.1 g Total Fat; 554 mg Sodium; 20 g Protein; 30 g Carbohydrate; 2 g Dietary Fiber

Pictured on front cover.

SPEEDY PIZZA

French bread, cut into layers, makes an ideal instant crust. Good snack food.

French bread loaf	1	1
Hard margarine (or butter), softened	3 tbsp.	50 mL
Chopped onion	1 cup	250 mL
Cooking oil	2 tsp.	10 mL
Tomato sauce	7½ oz.	213 mL
Dried whole oregano	½ tsp.	2 mL
Dried sweet basil	½ tsp.	2 mL
Garlic powder	¼ tsp.	1 mL
Salt	¼ tsp	1 mL
Pepper	⅛ tsp.	0.5 mL
Chopped salami, summer sausage or pepperoni (or all three)	1½ cups	375 mL
Grated Parmesan cheese	¼ cup	60 mL
Mozzarella cheese slices (can use more)	6	6

Slice loaf lengthwise into 2 halves. Brush margarine on cut sides. Place on ungreased baking sheet.

Sauté onion in cooking oil in medium frying pan until soft.

Stir next 6 ingredients together in small bowl. Spread over loaf halves. Divide onion over each.

Scatter meat over each. Sprinkle with Parmesan cheese. Arrange mozzarella cheese slices over top. Bake on bottom rack in 350°F (175°C) oven for about 20 minutes. Cuts into 6 thick slices each, making 12 slices in total.

1 slice: 259 Calories; 13 g Total Fat; 725 mg Sodium; 11 g Protein; 25 g Carbohydrate; 1 g Dietary Fiber

Deli Meat Pizzas

PEPPERONI PLUS PIZZA

Lots of toppings as well as lots of flavor.

Pizza crust dough, your choice, pages 115 to 130 (or partially baked commercial)	1	1
Cooking oil	1 tsp.	5 mL
Chopped onion	1 cup	250 mL
Medium green pepper, chopped	1	1
Basic Pizza Sauce, page 132 (or other)	⅔ cup	150 mL
Grated part-skim mozzarella cheese	¾ cup	175 mL
Chopped fresh mushrooms	1 cup	250 mL
Thinly sliced pepperoni (2 inch, 5 cm, diameter), about 4 oz. (113 g)	1 cup	250 mL
Chopped cooked ham	½ cup	125 mL
Grated part-skim mozzarella cheese	¾ cup	175 mL
Sliced pitted ripe olives	¼ cup	60 mL

Prepare pizza dough. Roll out and press in greased 12 inch (30 cm) pizza pan, forming rim around edge.

Heat cooking oil in medium frying pan. Add onion and green pepper. Sauté until soft.

Spread sauce over crust. Sprinkle with first amount of mozzarella cheese, mushrooms, pepperoni, ham, green pepper mixture, second amount of mozzarella cheese and olives. Bake on bottom rack in 425°F (220°C) oven for 13 to 15 minutes, or for about 8 minutes if using partially baked crust. Cuts into 8 wedges.

1 wedge: 352 Calories; 17.9 g Total Fat; 823 mg Sodium; 16 g Protein; 32 g Carbohydrate; 2 g Dietary Fiber

HAWAIIAN PIZZA

Use a mild sauce for this delicious pizza so as not to overpower the delicate flavors. Very pretty.

Pizza crust dough, your choice, pages 115 to 130 (or partially baked commercial)	1	1
Favorite Tomato Pizza Sauce, page 138 (or other)	½ cup	125 mL
Grated part-skim mozzarella cheese	1 cup	250 mL
Canned pineapple tidbits, drained	14 oz.	398 mL
Diced cooked ham	1 cup	250 mL
Grated part-skim mozzarella cheese	½ cup	125 mL

(continued on next page)

Deli Meat Pizzas

Prepare pizza dough. Roll out and press in greased 12 inch (30 cm) pizza pan, forming rim around edge.

Spread sauce over crust. Sprinkle with first amount of cheese. Scatter pineapple and ham over top. Sprinkle second amount of cheese over all. Bake on bottom rack in 425°F (220°C) oven for 17 to 20 minutes, or for about 12 minutes if using partially baked crust. Cuts into 8 wedges.

1 wedge: 274 Calories; 9.7 g Total Fat; 556 mg Sodium; 13 g Protein; 33 g Carbohydrate; 2 g Dietary Fiber

---

HAM PIZZA

This begins with a very tasty sauce.

Pizza crust dough, your choice, pages 115 to 130 (or partially baked commercial)	1	1
Light salad dressing (or mayonnaise)	²/₃ cup	150 mL
Prepared mustard	1 tbsp.	15 mL
Prepared horseradish	2 tsp.	10 mL
Grated part-skim mozzarella cheese	³/₄ cup	175 mL
Cooked ham, ¼ inch (6 mm) thick, cut into ½ inch (12 mm) squares (or smaller)	½ lb.	225 g
Grated part-skim mozzarella cheese	³/₄ cup	175 mL

Prepare pizza dough. Roll out and press in greased 12 inch (30 cm) pizza pan, forming rim around edge.

Mix next 3 ingredients in small bowl. Spread over crust.

Layer remaining 3 ingredients in order given. Bake on bottom rack in 425°F (220°C) oven for 15 minutes, or for 10 minutes if using partially baked crust. Cuts into 8 wedges.

1 wedge: 324 Calories; 15.8 g Total Fat; 749 mg Sodium; 14 g Protein; 30 g Carbohydrate; 1 g Dietary Fiber

HAM AND GREEN PEPPER PIZZA: Add 1 chopped or sliced green pepper, raw or sautéed.

HAM AND ONION PIZZA: Add 1 cup (250 mL) chopped or sliced onion, sautéed until soft.

PEPPERONI SOLO PIZZA

Mainly cheese and pepperoni which bring out the best in each other.

Confetti Biscuit Pizza Crust dough, page 130 (or other biscuit crust)	1	1
Basic Pizza Sauce, page 132 (or other)	⅔ **cup**	150 mL
Grated part-skim mozzarella cheese	1 **cup**	250 mL
Thinly sliced pepperoni (2 inch, 5 cm, diameter)	1½ **cups**	375 mL
Grated part-skim mozzarella cheese	½ **cup**	125 mL

Prepare pizza dough. Roll out and press in greased 12 inch (30 cm) pizza pan, forming rim around edge.

Spread sauce over crust.

Sprinkle first amount of cheese over sauce. Add layer of pepperoni. Top with second amount of cheese. Bake on bottom rack in 425°F (220°C) oven for 13 to 15 minutes. Cuts into 8 wedges.

1 wedge: 359 Calories; 19.9 g Total Fat; 858 mg Sodium; 15 g Protein; 29 g Carbohydrate; 2 g Dietary Fiber

Pictured on front cover.

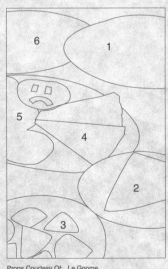

1. Merry-Go-Round Salad Pizza, page 148
   (on Biscuit Pizza Crust)
2. Sweet Ending Pizza, page 92
3. Muffin Pizza Appetizers, page 10
4. S'Getti And Meatball Pizza, page 28
5. Halloween Pizzas, page 20
6. Grasshopper Pizza, page 78

Props Courtesy Of: Le Gnome
Stokes
The Bay

So appealing looking with its orange-yellow topping with bits of broccoli and ham showing through.

Pizza crust dough, your choice, pages 115 to 130 (or partially baked commercial)	1	1
Broccoli florets	**2 cups**	**500 mL**
Boiling water, to cover		
Light cream cheese, softened	**4 oz.**	**125 g**
Prepared mustard	**2 tbsp.**	**30 mL**
Prepared horseradish	**1 tsp.**	**5 mL**
Cooked ham, ¼ inch (6 mm) thick, cut into ½ inch (12 mm) pieces (or smaller)	**½ lb.**	**225 g**
Chopped green onion	**2 tbsp.**	**30 mL**
Grated medium Cheddar cheese	**¾ cup**	**175 mL**
Grated part-skim mozzarella cheese	**¾ cup**	**175 mL**

Prepare pizza dough. Roll out and press in greased 12 inch (30 cm) pizza pan, forming rim around edge.

Cook broccoli in boiling water in medium saucepan until tender-crisp. Do not overcook. Drain.

Mash cream cheese, mustard and horseradish together in small bowl until smooth. Spread over crust. Scatter broccoli over top.

Top with ham and green onion.

Toss Cheddar cheese and mozzarella cheese together in small bowl. Sprinkle over top. Bake on bottom rack in 425°F (220°C) oven for 13 to 15 minutes, or for about 8 minutes if using partially baked crust. Let stand for 5 to 10 minutes before cutting to allow cream cheese to firm up a bit. Cuts into 8 wedges.

1 wedge: 321 Calories; 15.2 g Total Fat; 786 mg Sodium; 17 g Protein; 29 g Carbohydrate; 2 g Dietary Fiber

Could the green giant be a seasick ogre?

CHERRY CHEESE PIZZA

This dessert pizza tastes like cherry cheesecake. Delicious crunchy crust.

Caramel Crunch Pizza Crust, page 76	1	1
Light cream cheese, softened	12 oz.	375 g
Icing (confectioner's) sugar	1 cup	250 mL
Frozen light whipped topping (in a tub), thawed	4 cups	1 L
Canned cherry pie filling	19 oz.	540 mL

Prepare and bake crust according to recipe. Cool.

Beat cream cheese and icing sugar together in large bowl until smooth and light.

Fold in whipped topping. Spread over crust up to ½ inch (12 mm) from edge. Chill thoroughly.

Spoon pie filling in dabs here and there over top to cover. Chill until ready to serve. Cuts into 12 wedges.

1 wedge: 404 Calories; 18 g Total Fat; 463 mg Sodium; 6 g Protein; 56 g Carbohydrate; 1 g Dietary Fiber

Pictured on page 53.

QUICK BROWNIE PIZZA

Quick, easy and impressive. Either choose one filling or let everyone choose their own.

BROWNIE PIZZA CRUST		
Brownie mix (16 oz., 440 g)	1	1
FILLING CHOICES		
Scoops strawberry ice cream with	12	12
strawberry sundae topping	¾ cup	175 mL
Scoops vanilla ice cream with	12	12
butterscotch sundae topping	¾ cup	175 mL
Scoops chocolate ice cream with	12	12
chocolate sundae topping	¾ cup	175 mL

(continued on next page)

Brownie Pizza Crust: Prepare brownie batter according to instructions on package. Spread in greased 12 inch (30 cm) pizza pan. Bake on center rack in 350°F (175°C) oven for 12 to 15 minutes. Wooden pick inserted in several places should come out clean but moist. Excellent if served warm with ice cream topping. Cool if not serving right away.

Filling Choices: Place wedges on plates. Top with your choice of ice cream and sundae topping. Cuts into 12 wedges.

1 wedge: 402 Calories; 17.6 g Total Fat; 184 mg Sodium; 5 g Protein; 59 g Carbohydrate; 0 g Dietary Fiber

LEMON CRANBERRY PIZZA

A layer of cranberry sauce is between the lemon filling and the crust. Delicious mixture. Not recommended for freezing.

GRAHAM CRUST

Hard margarine (or butter)	½ cup	125 mL
Graham cracker crumbs	2 cups	500 mL
Brown sugar, packed	¼ cup	60 mL

FILLING

Water	2¾ cups	675 mL
Lemon pie filling (not prepared), enough for 2 pies	2 x 4 oz.	2 x 113 g
Granulated sugar	½ cup	125 mL
Water	½ cup	125 mL
Large eggs, fork-beaten	2	2
Whole cranberry sauce	14 oz.	398 mL

Graham Crust: Melt margarine in medium saucepan. Stir in graham crumbs and brown sugar. Measure out 2 tbsp. (30 mL) and set aside for topping. Press remaining graham crumbs in ungreased 12 inch (30 cm) pizza pan, forming rim around edge. Bake on center rack in 350°F (175°C) oven for 10 minutes. Cool.

Filling: Heat water in medium saucepan until boiling. Mix next 4 ingredients in small bowl. Stir into boiling water until it returns to a boil and thickens. Place saucepan in cold water, stirring often, to prevent lumps as it cools quickly to lukewarm.

Spread cranberry sauce over crust. Spoon lemon mixture over top, smoothing to cover completely. Sprinkle reserved graham crumbs over top. Chill until ready to serve. Cuts into 12 wedges.

1 wedge: 342 Calories; 10.9 g Total Fat; 303 mg Sodium; 3 g Protein; 61 g Carbohydrate; 1 g Dietary Fiber

A DREAM PIZZA

And a dream to eat. A smooth as satin filling over a crunchy base.

CARAMEL CRUNCH PIZZA CRUST

All-purpose flour	1½ cups	375 mL
Brown sugar, packed	½ cup	125 mL
Baking powder	1 tsp.	5 mL
Salt	¼ tsp.	1 mL
Hard margarine (or butter), softened	½ cup	125 mL
Egg yolks (large)	2	2
Vanilla	1 tsp.	5 mL

TOPPING

Egg whites (large), room temperature	2	2
Brown sugar, packed	1½ cups	375 mL
Cold water	⅓ cup	75 mL
Light corn syrup	1½ tsp.	7 mL
Maple flavoring	½ tsp.	2 mL
Chopped pecans	¾ cup	175 mL

Caramel Crunch Pizza Crust: Mix all 5 ingredients in medium bowl until crumbly.

Add egg yolks and vanilla. Mix well. Press in ungreased 12 inch (30 cm) pizza pan, forming rim around edge. Bake on center rack in 350°F (175°C) oven for 15 minutes. Cool.

Topping: Put first 5 ingredients into top of double boiler. Beat together well to mix. Place over boiling water in bottom. Beat constantly on low while it cooks for about 7 minutes or until egg white mixture stand in peaks when beater is raised. Remove from heat.

Fold in pecans. Spread over crust. Cool. Cuts into 12 wedges.

1 wedge: 346 Calories; 14.4 g Total Fat; 176 mg Sodium; 3 g Protein; 52 g Carbohydrate; 1 g Dietary Fiber

Cross a raccoon and a kangaroo and you get a fur coat with pockets.

A layer of chocolate is between the top layer and crust. Looks great garnished with chocolate and/or whipped topping.

SHORTBREAD PIZZA CRUST

All-purpose flour	2 cups	500 mL
Icing (confectioner's) sugar	½ cup	125 mL
Hard margarine (or butter), softened	1 cup	250 mL

FILLING

Semisweet chocolate chips	1½ cups	375 mL
Milk	¼ cup	60 mL

TOPPING

Creamed cottage cheese	2 cups	500 mL
Milk	1½ cups	375 mL
Vanilla pudding powder (not instant), 6 serving size	1	1
Cornstarch	2 tbsp.	30 mL
Granulated sugar	1 tbsp.	15 mL
Salt	¼ tsp.	1 mL
Milk	½ cup	125 mL

Shortbread Pizza Crust: Mix all 3 ingredients in medium bowl until crumbly. Using floured fingers, press in non-stick 12 inch (30 cm) pizza pan, forming rim around edge. Bake on center rack in 350°F (175°C) oven for 15 minutes. Cool.

Filling: Combine chocolate chips and milk in small saucepan. Heat over low, stirring often, until chocolate chips are melted. Cool until lukewarm. Pour over crust. Smooth to inside rim edge. Chill.

Topping: Measure cottage cheese and first amount of milk into blender. Process until smooth. Transfer to medium saucepan. Heat until boiling.

Stir pudding powder, cornstarch, sugar and salt together in separate medium bowl. Gradually add second amount of milk, stirring until smooth. Stir into boiling cottage cheese mixture until it returns to a boil and thickens. Place saucepan in cold water, stirring often, to prevent lumps as it cools quickly to lukewarm. Pour over chocolate. Spread evenly. Chill. Cuts into 12 wedges.

1 wedge: 447 Calories; 24.1 g Total Fat; 479 mg Sodium; 10 g Protein; 51 g Carbohydrate; 2 g Dietary Fiber

Pictured on page 53.

GRASSHOPPER PIZZA

Lime green in color. Very refreshing to eat.

Chocolate Pizza Crust dough, page 79	1	1
Lime-flavored gelatin (jelly powder)	2 × 3 oz.	2 × 85 g
Boiling water	1 cup	250 mL
Vanilla ice cream	1 cup	250 mL
Green Crème de Menthe liqueur	¼ cup	60 mL
Frozen light whipped topping (in a tub), thawed	2 cups	500 mL
Chocolate chips (or grated chocolate or chocolate curls), for garnish		

Prepare pizza dough. Press in ungreased 12 inch (30 cm) pizza pan, forming rim around edge. Bake on center rack in 350°F (175°C) oven for 10 minutes. Cool.

Empty gelatin into medium bowl. Add boiling water. Stir together until gelatin is dissolved.

Add ice cream. Stir until melted. Add Crème de Menthe. Stir. Chill, stirring and scraping down sides occasionally, until mixture is like thick syrup.

Add whipped topping. Fold in until no white streaks remain. Pour over crust.

Garnish with chocolate chips. Chill until firm and ready to serve. Cuts into 12 wedges.

1 wedge: 302 Calories; 15.7 g Total Fat; 393 mg Sodium; 3 g Protein; 37 g Carbohydrate; trace Dietary Fiber

Pictured on page 71.

Paré Pointer

Cross a sheep and a porcupine and you will have an animal that will knit its own scarves.

Dessert Pizzas

STRAWBERRY CREAM PIZZA

A pretty pink topping over vanilla ice cream on a chocolate crust. Great to keep on hand in the freezer.

CHOCOLATE PIZZA CRUST

Hard margarine (or butter)	½ cup	125 mL
Chocolate wafer (or cookie) crumbs	2 cups	500 mL
Granulated sugar	2 tbsp.	30 mL

TOPPING

Vanilla ice cream, softened	4 cups	1 L
Egg white (large)	1	1
Granulated sugar	6 tbsp.	100 mL
Frozen sliced strawberries in syrup, partly thawed (see Note)	½ x 15 oz.	½ x 425 g
Lemon juice	1 tbsp.	15 mL
Frozen light whipped topping (in a tub), thawed	2 cups	500 mL

Chocolate Pizza Crust: Melt margarine in medium saucepan. Stir in wafer crumbs and sugar. Reserve 2 tbsp. (30 mL) mixture. Press remaining mixture in ungreased 12 inch (30 cm) pizza pan, forming rim around edge. Bake on center rack in 350°F (175°C) oven for 10 minutes. Cool.

Topping: Spread ice cream over crust to within ½ inch (12 mm) of edge. Freeze.

Combine egg white, sugar, strawberries and lemon juice in medium bowl. Beat on high until thickened and volume has increased. Fold in whipped topping. Spread over ice cream. Sprinkle with reserved wafer crumbs. Freeze. Cuts into 12 wedges.

Note: Cut package in half while still frozen using serrated knife.

1 wedge: 342 Calories; 19.5 g Total Fat; 223 mg Sodium; 3 g Protein; 42 g Carbohydrate; 1 g Dietary Fiber

Paré Pointer

Did the apple turnover because it saw the cheese roll?

FRUIT PIZZA

A real beauty with flavor to match.

EASY SUGAR PIZZA CRUST

All-purpose flour	1¼ cups	300 mL
Granulated sugar	½ cup	125 mL
Hard margarine (or butter), softened	⅔ cup	150 mL

TOPPING

Light cream cheese, softened	8 oz.	250 g
Icing (confectioner's) sugar	⅓ cup	75 mL
Vanilla	1 tsp.	5 mL
Fresh blueberries	18-24	18-24
Fresh strawberries, halved lengthwise	12	12
Canned mandarin oranges, well drained	12 oz.	341 mL
Kiwifruit, peeled and sliced	6-8	6-8

GLAZE

Apricot (or peach) jam	¼ cup	60 mL
Water	1 tbsp.	15 mL

Easy Sugar Pizza Crust: Mix all 3 ingredients in medium bowl until ball is formed. Press in ungreased 12 inch (30 cm) pizza pan, forming rim around edge. Bake on center rack in 350°F (175°C) oven for about 12 minutes. Cool.

Topping: Beat cream cheese, icing sugar and vanilla together in small bowl until smooth. Spread over crust.

Arrange fruit to make an attractive pattern.

Glaze: Stir jam and water together in small cup. Rub through sieve. Dab onto fruit using pastry brush. Chill. Cuts into 12 wedges.

1 wedge: 293 Calories; 14.8 g Total Fat; 330 mg Sodium; 4 g Protein; 37 g Carbohydrate; 2 g Dietary Fiber

Pictured on front cover.

CHOCOLATE PEAR PIZZA

This can only get better with more chocolate drizzled over top.

PASTRY PIZZA CRUST

All-purpose flour	1⅓ cups	325 mL
Granulated sugar	2 tbsp.	30 mL
Baking powder	¼ tsp.	1 mL
Salt	¼ tsp.	1 mL
Hard margarine (or butter)	½ cup	125 mL
Large egg	1	1
Cold water	1 tbsp.	15 mL

TOPPING

Prepared non-fat vanilla pudding (lunch size)	5 oz.	142 g
Canned pears, drained, thinly sliced and blotted dry	2 x 14 oz.	2 x 398 mL

GLAZE

Semisweet chocolate chips	¼ cup	60 mL
Hard margarine (or butter)	1 tbsp.	15 mL
Maraschino cherries, halved	12	12

Pastry Pizza Crust: Combine flour, sugar, baking powder and salt in medium bowl. Cut in margarine until mixture is crumbly.

Beat egg and cold water together with fork in small cup. Add to flour mixture. Stir together to make soft ball. Turn out onto lightly floured surface. Roll large enough to fit 12 inch (30 cm) pizza pan. Place in ungreased pizza pan, crimping edge nicely. Bake on center rack in 400°F (205°C) oven for about 10 minutes until golden. Cool.

Topping: Spread pudding over crust up to ½ inch (12 mm) from edge. Arrange pear slices over pudding. Chill.

Glaze: Melt chocolate chips and margarine in small saucepan over low, stirring often. Turn into freezer bag. Snip off a small bit from corner. Drizzle decoratively over pears shortly before serving.

Place cherry halves here and there for color. Cuts into 12 wedges.

1 wedge: 201 Calories; 10.8 g Total Fat; 194 mg Sodium; 3 g Protein; 24 g Carbohydrate; 2 g Dietary Fiber

APPLE PIZZA

Totally awesome! You won't miss the pastry.

APPLE FILLING

Peeled, cored and sliced apple	6 cups	1.5 L
Granulated sugar	1 cup	250 mL
Ground cinnamon	3/4 tsp.	4 mL
Lemon juice	1 tsp.	5 mL
Salt	1/8 tsp.	0.5 mL
Minute tapioca	2 tbsp.	30 mL

SWEET BISCUIT MIX PIZZA CRUST

Biscuit mix	2 cups	500 mL
Granulated sugar	4 tsp.	20 mL
Milk, scant measure	1/2 cup	125 mL
Cooking oil	1 tsp.	5 mL

TOPPING

All-purpose flour	1 cup	250 mL
Brown sugar, packed	1/2 cup	125 mL
Ground cinnamon	1/4 tsp.	1 mL
Salt	1/4 tsp.	1 mL
Hard margarine (or butter), softened	6 tbsp.	100 mL

Apple Filling: Combine apple and sugar in large saucepan. Let stand until juice begins to form.

Add cinnamon, lemon juice, salt and tapioca. Stir together. Heat, stirring often, until boiling. Boil gently for about 6 minutes until apple slices are just tender-crisp. More cooking takes place in oven. Remove from heat. Let stand for 5 to 10 minutes before putting onto crust.

Sweet Biscuit Mix Pizza Crust: Measure biscuit mix, sugar and milk into medium bowl. Mix to form soft ball. Knead on lightly floured surface 8 times. Using floured hands, press in greased 12 inch (30 cm) pizza pan, forming rim around edge.

Brush crust with cooking oil. Spread apple mixture over top.

Topping: Mix all 5 ingredients in small bowl until crumbly. Sprinkle over apple filling. Bake on center rack in 400°F (205°C) oven for about 20 minutes. Cuts into 12 wedges.

1 wedge: 344 Calories; 9.5 g Total Fat; 456 mg Sodium; 3 g Protein; 63 g Carbohydrate; 2 g Dietary Fiber

APPLE PIE PIZZA: Prepare premix pie dough (enough for double crust pie), or Pastry Pizza Crust dough, page 81. Roll out and fit in ungreased 12 inch (30 cm) pizza pan, forming rim around edge. Spread with Apple Filling and Topping, above. Bake as above.

Deep golden color. Raisins peek through the top. This is good with or without the icing. Or try the variation with the butterscotch chips.

Raisins	1 cup	250 mL
Water	1/2 cup	125 mL
Hard margarine (or butter), softened	1/2 cup	125 mL
Brown sugar, packed	1/2 cup	125 mL
Granulated sugar	1/2 cup	125 mL
Large eggs	2	2
Vanilla	1 tsp.	5 mL
All-purpose flour	2 cups	500 mL
Baking powder	1/2 tsp.	2 mL
Baking soda	1/2 tsp.	2 mL
Salt	3/4 tsp.	4 mL
Ground cinnamon	1/2 tsp.	2 mL
Ground nutmeg	1/4 tsp.	1 mL
Chopped walnuts (or pecans)	3/4 cup	175 mL
ICING		
Hard margarine (or butter)	1/4 cup	60 mL
Brown sugar, packed	1/2 cup	125 mL
Milk	2 tbsp.	30 mL
Icing (confectioner's) sugar	1 cup	250 mL
Chopped walnuts, optional	1/4 cup	60 mL

Boil raisins gently in water in small saucepan for 5 minutes. Cool. Do not drain.

Cream margarine and both sugars together in medium bowl. Beat in eggs, 1 at a time. Add vanilla. Add raisins and water. Mix.

Add next 7 ingredients. Stir together well. Press in greased 12 inch (30 cm) pizza pan. Bake on center rack in 375°F (190°C) oven for about 15 minutes. Cool.

Icing: Combine margarine, brown sugar and milk in small saucepan. Bring to a boil. Simmer for 2 minutes. Cool.

Stir in icing sugar. If too stiff, add a bit more milk until soft enough to spread. If too thin, add more icing sugar. Spread over top of cookie pizza. Sprinkle with walnuts. Cuts into 16 wedges.

Variation: Sprinkle hot pizza with 1 cup (250 mL) good quality butterscotch chips. Let stand until melted. Spread or swirl with tip of knife.

1 wedge: 304 Calories; 13.5 g Total Fat; 289 mg Sodium; 4 g Protein; 50 g Carbohydrate; 1 g Dietary Fiber

Pictured on page 53.

PIZZA FLAN

A thick cake-like crust covered with a vanilla pudding layer then decorated with fruit.

CAKE PIZZA CRUST

Hard margarine (or butter), softened	6 tbsp.	100 mL
Granulated sugar	½ cup	125 mL
Large eggs	2	2
All-purpose flour	1¾ cups	425 mL
Baking powder	1½ tsp.	7 mL
Salt	⅛ tsp.	0.5 mL

FILLING

Milk	2¾ cups	675 mL
Vanilla pudding powder (not instant), 6 serving size	1	1
Cornstarch	2 tbsp.	30 mL
Milk	⅓ cup	75 mL

TOPPING

Cantaloupe balls	12	12
Strawberries, halved lengthwise	6	6
Honeydew balls	6	6

GLAZE

Water	1 tbsp.	15 mL
Apple jelly	¼ cup	60 mL
Frozen light whipped topping (in a tub), thawed	1 cup	250 mL

Cake Pizza Crust: Cream margarine and sugar together in medium bowl. Beat in eggs, 1 at a time.

Add flour, baking powder and salt. Stir just to moisten. Spread in greased 12 inch (30 cm) deep dish pizza pan. Bake on center rack in 350°F (175°C) oven for 18 to 20 minutes. Wooden pick inserted in several places should come out clean. Cool.

Filling: Heat first amount of milk in medium saucepan until boiling.

Stir pudding powder and cornstarch together in small bowl. Mix in second amount of milk. Stir into boiling milk until boiling and thickened. Place saucepan in cold water, stirring often, to prevent lumps as it cools quickly to lukewarm. Pour over crust. Cool completely.

(continued on next page)

Topping: Place cantaloupe balls near outside edge of crust. Place strawberries around middle section. Place honeydew balls closer to center.

Glaze: Stir water and jelly together in small saucepan over medium until melted. Dab onto fruit using pastry brush. Spoon dabs of topping around outside edge. Chill. Cuts into 12 wedges.

1 wedge: 300 Calories; 8.6 g Total Fat; 188 mg Sodium; 6 g Protein; 51 g Carbohydrate; 1 g Dietary Fiber

Pictured on page 53.

CHOCOLATE CHIP PIZZA

A good dessert as is but exceptionally good when iced.

Hard margarine (or butter), softened	¾ cup	175 mL
Brown sugar, packed	¾ cup	175 mL
Granulated sugar	¼ cup	60 mL
Large eggs	2	2
Vanilla	1 tsp.	5 mL
All-purpose flour	2 cups	500 mL
Cornstarch	¼ cup	60 mL
Baking soda	1 tsp.	5 mL
Baking powder	½ tsp.	2 mL
Salt	¾ tsp.	4 mL
Semisweet chocolate chips	1½ cups	375 mL

Cream margarine and both sugars together in large bowl. Beat in eggs, 1 at a time. Add vanilla. Beat together well.

Add remaining 6 ingredients. Stir together. Press in greased 12 inch (30 cm) pizza pan. Bake on center rack in 350°F (175°C) oven for 12 to 15 minutes. Cuts into 12 wedges.

1 wedge: 379 Calories; 19.9 g Total Fat; 446 mg Sodium; 4 g Protein; 49 g Carbohydrate; 2 g Dietary Fiber

TRIPLE CHOCOLATE CHIP PIZZA: Sprinkle hot baked Chocolate Chip Pizza, above, with ⅓ cup (75 mL) each semisweet chocolate chips, butterscotch chips and white chocolate chips. When melted, spread with knife in zigzag pattern. Cuts into 12 wedges.

RED SPOKE PIZZA

Use any red jam for this. Easy, yet so impressive.

Hard margarine (or butter), softened	½ cup	125 mL
Brown sugar, packed	1 cup	250 mL
Large egg	1	1
Milk	½ cup	125 mL
Vanilla	1 tsp.	5 mL
All-purpose flour	3 cups	750 mL
Baking powder	1 tbsp.	15 mL
Salt	½ tsp.	2 mL
Raspberry jam, sieved if desired	¼ cup	60 mL

Cream margarine and brown sugar together in large bowl. Beat in egg. Add milk and vanilla. Beat together well.

Add flour, baking powder and salt. Mix. Press in greased 12 inch (30 cm) pizza pan. Mark top lightly with knife, making 12 wedges. With side of your hand, using baby finger, press to indent down center of each wedge, beginning ¾ inch (2 cm) from edge and ending 1½ inches (3.8 cm) from center.

Spread jam in indentations. Bake on center rack in 350°F (175°C) oven for 13 to 16 minutes. Cuts into 12 wedges.

1 wedge: *298 Calories; 9 g Total Fat; 231 mg Sodium; 4 g Protein; 50 g Carbohydrate; 1 g Dietary Fiber*

Pictured on page 53.

BLONDIE PIZZA

Serve this warm with a scoop of ice cream for the finishing touch.

Hard margarine (or butter), softened	½ cup	125 mL
Brown sugar, packed	1½ cups	375 mL
Large eggs	2	2
Vanilla	1 tsp.	5 mL
All-purpose flour	1½ cups	375 mL
Baking powder	1 tsp.	5 mL
Salt	¼ tsp.	1 mL
Chopped walnuts (or pecans)	½ cup	125 mL
Butterscotch chips	⅓ cup	75 mL
Chocolate miniature semisweet chips	½ cup	125 mL

(continued on next page)

Cream margarine and brown sugar together in large bowl. Beat in eggs, 1 at a time. Add vanilla. Mix.

Add remaining 6 ingredients. Stir just to moisten. Press in greased 12 inch (30 cm) pizza pan. Bake on center rack in 350°F (175°C) oven for 18 to 20 minutes. Cuts into 12 wedges.

1 wedge: *348 Calories; 15 g Total Fat; 179 mg Sodium; 4 g Protein; 52 g Carbohydrate; 1 g Dietary Fiber*

LEMON PIZZA DESSERT

An almost white dessert. Fluffy and rich tasting. Just a hint of lemon.

SWEET PIZZA CRUST

Hard margarine (or butter), softened	1 cup	250 mL
All-purpose flour	2 cups	500 mL
Icing (confectioner's) sugar	½ cup	125 mL

FILLING

Light cream cheese, softened	8 oz.	250 g
Icing (confectioner's) sugar	½ cup	125 mL
Milk	½ cup	125 mL
Non-fat sour cream	½ cup	125 mL
Lemon juice	¼ cup	60 mL
Instant vanilla pudding powder (4 serving size)	1	1
Envelopes dessert topping (prepared according to package directions)	2	2

Sweet Pizza Crust: Mix all 3 ingredients in medium bowl until crumbly. Press in ungreased 12 inch (30 cm) pizza pan. Bake on center rack in 325°F (160°C) oven for about 20 minutes until golden. Cool.

Filling: Beat cream cheese, icing sugar and milk together in large bowl until smooth. Add sour cream and lemon juice. Mix well. Add pudding powder. Beat for 30 seconds.

Fold dessert topping into cheese mixture. Spread over crust. Chill. Cuts into 12 wedges.

1 wedge: *390 Calories; 22.9 g Total Fat; 434 mg Sodium; 6 g Protein; 42 g Carbohydrate; 1 g Dietary Fiber*

MUD PIE PIZZA

Ready to serve directly from the freezer, this crispy crust has an ice cream filling with a chocolate topping.

Chocolate Pizza Crust dough, page 79	1	1
Coffee ice cream, softened slightly (see Note)	4 cups	1 L
Skim evaporated milk	¼ cup	60 mL
Semisweet chocolate chips	1 cup	250 mL
Instant coffee granules	1 tsp.	5 mL
Hot water	2 tsp.	10 mL

Prepare pizza dough. Press in ungreased 12 inch (30 cm) pizza pan. Bake on center rack in 350°F (175°C) oven for 10 minutes. Cool.

Spread ice cream over crust. Freeze.

Heat evaporated milk and chocolate chips in small saucepan over low, stirring often.

Dissolve coffee granules in hot water in small cup. Stir into chocolate mixture. Spread over ice cream. Freeze. Cuts into 12 wedges.

1 wedge: 354 Calories; 22.3 g Total Fat; 306 mg Sodium; 5 g Protein; 39 g Carbohydrate; 2 g Dietary Fiber

Note: If coffee ice cream is not available, dissolve 2 tsp. (10 mL) instant coffee granules in 4 tsp. (20 mL) hot water. Cool, then mix into 4 cups (1 L) softened vanilla ice cream.

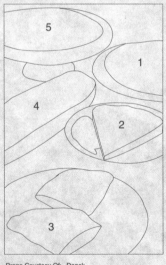

1. Barbecued Chicken Pizza, page 52
   (on Basic Pizza Crust)
2. Baked Alaska Pizza, page 91
3. Ham And Cheese Calzones, page 48
   (using Calzone Pizza Crust)
4. Loaf Of Pizza, page 37
5. Chicken Caesar Salad Pizza, page 147
   (on Biscuit Pizza Crust)

Props Courtesy Of: Dansk
Le Gnome
Stokes
The Bay

Prepare and assemble ahead of time and freeze. Bake and serve at the last minute.

CHOCO CAKE PIZZA CRUST

All-purpose flour	1¼ cups	300 mL
Granulated sugar	1 cup	250 mL
Cocoa	¼ cup	60 mL
Hard margarine (or butter), softened	¼ cup	60 mL
Baking powder	1 tsp.	5 mL
Baking soda	1 tsp.	5 mL
Salt	½ tsp.	2 mL
Large egg	1	1
Vanilla	1 tsp.	5 mL
Hot water	1 cup	250 mL

TOPPING

Neapolitan ice cream	1½ qts.	1.5 L
Chocolate sundae topping	⅓ cup	75 mL
Strawberry sundae topping	¼ cup	60 mL
Butterscotch sundae topping	¼ cup	60 mL

MERINGUE

Egg whites (large), room temperature	6	6
Cream of tartar	½ tsp.	2 mL
Granulated sugar	1⅛ cups	280 mL

Choco Cake Pizza Crust: Measure all 10 ingredients into large bowl. Beat together until smooth. Spread in greased 12 inch (30 cm) pizza pan. Bake on center rack in 350°F (175°C) oven for about 15 minutes. Wooden pick inserted near center should come out clean. Cool thoroughly.

Topping: Slice ice cream 1 inch (2.5 cm) thick. Leaving 1 inch (2.5 cm) cake border, layer ice cream over top. Fill in spaces. Freeze.

Drizzle 3 circles of sundae topping on top of ice cream: chocolate in ring around outside edge, strawberry in ring halfway in from edge and caramel in middle. Freeze, being careful to keep pizza level.

Meringue: Beat egg whites and cream of tartar together in medium bowl until soft peaks form. Gradually beat in sugar until sugar is dissolved and egg whites are stiff. Spoon over ice cream and cake to cover top and sides completely. Freeze. When ready to serve, bake on center rack in 450°F (230°C) oven for about 4 minutes until golden. Serve immediately. Cuts into 12 wedges.

1 wedge: 451 Calories; 13.6 g Total Fat; 395 mg Sodium; 7 g Protein; 78 g Carbohydrate; 2 g Dietary Fiber

Pictured on page 89.

SWEET ENDING PIZZA

A soft peanut butter cookie crust, covered with chocolate and then topped with candy-coated chocolate. Festive.

Smooth peanut butter	¾ cup	175 mL
Hard margarine (or butter), softened	½ cup	125 mL
Brown sugar, packed	1 cup	250 mL
Granulated sugar	¼ cup	60 mL
Large eggs	2	2
Vanilla	1 tsp.	5 mL
All-purpose flour	1¾ cups	425 mL
Baking soda	¾ tsp.	4 mL
Baking powder	½ tsp.	2 mL
Salt	½ tsp.	2 mL
Semisweet chocolate chips	½ cup	125 mL
Butterscotch chips	½ cup	125 mL
Candy-coated chocolate candies	½ cup	125 mL

Cream peanut butter and margarine together in large bowl. Beat in both sugars. Beat in eggs, 1 at a time. Add vanilla. Mix.

Add flour, baking soda, baking powder and salt. Stir just to moisten. Press in greased 12 inch (30 cm) pizza pan. Bake on center rack in 350°F (175°C) oven for 7 to 9 minutes until lightly browned.

Sprinkle hot pizza with both kinds of chips. Let stand to soften. Draw knife back and forth over top to smooth out most chips.

Scatter candies over top, pressing down lightly into melted chips. Cool. Cuts into 16 wedges.

1 wedge: 342 Calories; 16.4 g Total Fat; 305 mg Sodium; 6 g Protein; 46 g Carbohydrate; 2 g Dietary Fiber

Pictured on page 71.

Paré Pointer

Did you know you get satisfaction from a satisfactory?

A tasty good chili flavor that you can easily add to if desired.

Basic Double Pizza Crust dough, page 116	1	1
Cooking oil	2 tsp.	10 mL
Chopped onion	1 cup	250 mL
Lean ground beef	1 lb.	454 g
Commercial enchilada sauce (or salsa)	¼ cup	60 mL
Grated medium Cheddar cheese	1½ cups	375 mL
Chili powder (or more to taste)	4 tsp.	20 mL
Salt	½ tsp.	2 mL
Pepper	¼ tsp.	1 mL
Chopped pitted ripe (or pimiento-stuffed green) olives (optional)	½ cup	125 mL

Prepare pizza dough. Divide into 2 equal balls. Roll out and press 1 ball in greased 12 inch (30 cm) pizza pan, forming rim around edge. Cover remaining ball with plastic wrap to keep from drying out.

Heat cooking oil in medium frying pan. Add onion and ground beef. Scramble-fry until beef is no longer pink.

Add next 6 ingredients. Stir together. Spread over crust. Roll out remaining ball of dough large enough to fit pan. Dampen edge with water. Fit crust over top. Crimp edge to seal. Make slits in top with tip of paring knife. Bake on bottom rack in 400°F (205°C) oven for about 20 minutes. Cuts into 8 wedges.

1 wedge: *474 Calories; 23.1 g Total Fat; 655 mg Sodium; 22 g Protein; 43 g Carbohydrate; 3 g Dietary Fiber*

Dinosaurs can build houses because they can really raise the roof.

STEW STUFFED PIZZA

A most unusual way to serve stew. Contains sausage meat. Spicy sausage may be used instead.

Basic Double Pizza Crust dough, page 116	1	1
Sausage meat	³/₄ lb.	340 g
Chopped onion	³/₄ cup	175 mL
Chopped fresh mushrooms	¹/₂ cup	125 mL
Diced carrot, ¹/₄ inch (6 mm)	¹/₂ cup	125 mL
Diced potato, ¹/₄ inch (6 mm)	¹/₂ cup	125 mL
Salt	¹/₂ tsp.	2 mL
Pepper	¹/₈ tsp.	0.5 mL
Water	¹/₂ cup	125 mL
Frozen peas	¹/₄ cup	60 mL
Reserved broth, plus water to make	¹/₂ cup	125 mL
Chicken bouillon powder	¹/₂ tsp.	2 mL
Water	2 tbsp.	30 mL
Cornstarch	4 tsp.	20 mL
Salt	¹/₄ tsp.	1 mL
Pepper	¹/₈ tsp.	0.5 mL
Basic Pizza Sauce, page 132 (or other)	¹/₂ cup	125 mL
Grated part-skim mozzarella cheese	³/₄ cup	175 mL

Prepare pizza dough. Divide into 2 equal balls. Roll out and press 1 ball in greased 12 inch (30 cm) pizza pan, forming rim around edge. Cover remaining ball with plastic wrap to keep from drying out.

Scramble-fry sausage meat, onion and mushrooms in medium frying pan until sausage meat is cooked.

Combine next 5 ingredients in medium saucepan. Simmer for 6 to 7 minutes.

Add peas. Simmer for 2 minutes. Drain and reserve liquid. Add sausage mixture. Stir together. Remove from heat.

(continued on next page)

Combine next 6 ingredients in small saucepan. Heat and stir until boiling and thickened. Stir into sausage mixture.

Spread sauce over crust in pan. Sprinkle cheese over sauce. Spoon stew mixture over cheese. Roll out remaining ball of dough large enough to fit pan. Dampen edge with water. Fit crust over top. Crimp edge to seal. Make slits in top with tip of paring knife. Bake on bottom rack in 400°F (205°C) oven for 20 to 25 minutes. Cuts into 8 wedges.

1 wedge: 477 Calories; 25 g Total Fat; 889 mg Sodium; 15 g Protein; 48 g Carbohydrate; 3 g Dietary Fiber

Pictured on page 143.

SPANAKOPITA PIZZA

This is a variation of span-a-KOH-pih-ta, a favorite in Greece.

Basic Double Pizza Crust dough, page 116	1	1
Basic Pizza Sauce, page 132 (or other)	½ cup	125 mL
Large egg	1	1
Frozen chopped spinach, thawed and squeezed dry	10 oz.	300 g
Onion flakes	¼ cup	60 mL
Crumbled feta cheese	½ cup	125 mL
Grated Parmesan cheese	1 tbsp.	15 mL
Grated part-skim mozzarella cheese	1 cup	250 mL

Prepare pizza dough. Divide into 2 equal balls. Roll out and press 1 ball in greased 12 inch (30 cm) pizza pan, forming rim around edge. Cover remaining ball with plastic wrap to keep from drying out.

Spread sauce over crust.

Beat egg with spoon in medium bowl until smooth. Add spinach, onion flakes, feta cheese and Parmesan cheese. Stir together well. Spoon over sauce.

Sprinkle with mozzarella cheese. Roll out remaining ball of dough large enough to fit pan. Dampen edge with water. Fit crust over top. Crimp edge to seal. Make slits in top with tip of paring knife. Bake on bottom rack in 400°F (205°C) oven for 20 to 25 minutes. Cuts into 8 wedges.

1 wedge: 329 Calories; 10.8 g Total Fat; 438 mg Sodium; 13 g Protein; 45 g Carbohydrate; 3 g Dietary Fiber

TOURTIÉRE PIZZA

An old favorite that has to be included in a pizza selection.

Double Biscuit Pizza Crust dough, page 128 (or Basic Double Pizza Crust dough, page 116)	1	1
Lean ground pork	1½ lbs.	680 g
Chopped onion	1¼ cups	300 mL
Salt	1 tsp.	5 mL
Garlic powder	½ tsp.	2 mL
Pepper	¼ tsp.	1 mL
Ground thyme	¼ tsp.	1 mL
Poultry seasoning	¼ tsp.	1 mL
Ground cloves	⅟₁₆ tsp.	0.5 mL
Small bay leaf	1	1
Water	2 cups	500 mL
Instant potato flakes	½ cup	125 mL
Grated part-skim mozzarella cheese	1 cup	250 mL

Prepare pizza dough. Divide dough into 2 equal balls. Roll out and press 1 ball in greased 12 inch (30 cm) pizza pan, forming rim around edge. Cover remaining ball with tea towel to keep from drying out.

Scramble-fry ground pork and onion in medium non-stick frying pan until onion is soft and pork is no longer pink. Drain. Cool.

Add next 8 ingredients. Stir together. Cover. Simmer for about 15 minutes. Discard bay leaf. Skim off fat.

Add potato flakes. Stir together until thickened.

Sprinkle crust with cheese. Spoon pork mixture over cheese. Smooth top. Roll out remaining ball of dough large enough to fit pan. Dampen edge with water. Fit crust over top. Crimp edge to seal. Make slits in top with tip of paring knife. Bake on bottom rack in 400°F (205°C) oven for 15 to 20 minutes until browned. Cuts into 8 wedges.

1 wedge: 435 Calories; 17.3 g Total Fat; 725 mg Sodium; 21 g Protein; 47 g Carbohydrate; 2 g Dietary Fiber

Flavor is mild and very good. Imagine you are on the bayou.

Rice Pizza Crust, page 122 (or other)	1	1
Hot Italian (or regular) sausage, cut into ¼ inch (6 mm) coins	6 oz.	170 g
Chopped green pepper	½ cup	125 mL
Chopped onion	½ cup	125 mL
Chopped celery	⅓ cup	75 mL
Cooking oil	2 tsp.	10 mL
Canned diced tomatoes, drained, juice reserved	½ cup	125 mL
Diced cooked ham	½ cup	125 mL
Cooked small or medium fresh (or frozen, thawed) shrimp	4 oz.	113 g
Reserved tomato juice	¼ cup	60 mL
Hot pepper sauce	½ tsp.	2 mL
Cornstarch	2 tsp.	10 mL
Basic Pizza Sauce, page 132 (or other)	¼ cup	60 mL
Grated part-skim mozzarella cheese	¾ cup	175 mL
Grated part-skim mozzarella cheese	¾ cup	175 mL

Prepare rice crust but do not bake.

Cook both sides of sausage coins in large frying pan. Drain. Place sausage in small bowl.

Combine next 4 ingredients in frying pan. Sauté until soft.

Add tomato, ham and shrimp. Add sausage. Stir together.

Mix tomato juice, hot pepper sauce and cornstarch in small cup. Pour over meat mixture. Heat and stir until thickened.

Spread sauce over crust. Sprinkle first amount of cheese over sauce. Spoon sausage mixture over cheese. Spread evenly. Sprinkle with second amount of cheese. Bake on bottom rack in 425°F (220°C) oven for 15 to 20 minutes. Cuts into 8 wedges.

1 wedge: *285 Calories; 9 g Total Fat; 424 mg Sodium; 16 g Protein; 34 g Carbohydrate; 2 g Dietary Fiber*

Pictured on page 143.

CRAB IMPERIAL PIZZA

A special pizza for special people. Delicious and impressive.

Pizza crust dough, your choice, pages 115 to 130 (or partially baked commercial)	1	1
Chili sauce	1/3 cup	75 mL
Sweet pickle relish	1½ tbsp.	25 mL
Prepared horseradish	¼ tsp.	1 mL
Worcestershire sauce	¼ tsp.	1 mL
All-purpose flour	2 tbsp.	30 mL
Dry mustard	½ tsp.	2 mL
Salt	½ tsp.	2 mL
Pepper	⅛ tsp.	0.5 mL
Cayenne pepper, just a pinch		
Parsley flakes	½ tsp.	2 mL
Skim evaporated milk	⅔ cup	150 mL
Hard margarine (or butter)	1 tbsp.	15 mL
Large egg, fork-beaten	1	1
Hard margarine (or butter), melted	2 tbsp.	30 mL
Dry bread crumbs	½ cup	125 mL
Grated part-skim mozzarella cheese	¾ cup	175 mL
Canned crabmeat, drained and cartilage removed	2 × 4 oz.	2 × 113 g

Prepare pizza dough. Roll out and press in greased 12 inch (30 cm) pizza pan, forming rim around edge.

Stir next 4 ingredients together in small bowl.

Mix next 6 ingredients in small saucepan. Gradually whisk in evaporated milk until no lumps remain. Heat and stir until mixture is boiling and thickened.

Add first amount of margarine. Stir until margarine is melted. Stir about ¼ cup (60 mL) hot mixture into egg in cup. Stir egg mixture back into saucepan. Stir until just barely starting to boil. Remove from heat.

Stir second amount of margarine and bread crumbs together in small cup.

(continued on next page)

Spread chili sauce mixture over crust. Sprinkle with cheese. Spoon mustard sauce over cheese. Scatter crabmeat over top. Sprinkle with bread crumb mixture. Bake on bottom rack in 425°F (220°C) oven for 13 to 15 minutes, or for 8 minutes if using partially baked crust. Cuts into 8 wedges.

1 wedge: 298 Calories; 10.9 g Total Fat; 621 mg Sodium; 10 g Protein; 39 g Carbohydrate; 2 g Dietary Fiber

SHRIMP AND MUSHROOM PIZZA

Shrimp lovers may want to add more shrimp, although it is well covered. Very good.

Pizza crust dough, your choice, pages 115 to 130 (or partially baked commercial)	1	1
Chili sauce	½ cup	125 mL
Prepared horseradish	2 tsp.	10 mL
Grated part-skim mozzarella cheese	1 cup	250 mL
Sliced fresh mushrooms	1 cup	250 mL
Cooked small fresh (or frozen, thawed) shrimp	½ lb.	225 g
Grated part-skim mozzarella cheese	½ cup	125 mL

Prepare pizza dough. Roll out and press in greased 12 inch (30 cm) pizza pan, forming rim around edge.

Stir chili sauce and horseradish together in small cup. Spread over crust.

Sprinkle with first amount of cheese. Layer with mushrooms, shrimp and second amount of cheese. Bake on bottom rack in 425°F (220°C) oven for 13 to 15 minutes, or for about 8 minutes if using partially baked crust. Cuts into 8 wedges.

1 wedge: 260 Calories; 7.8 g Total Fat; 499 mg Sodium; 16 g Protein; 31 g Carbohydrate; 2 g Dietary Fiber

Pictured on page 125.

FESTIVE SALMON PIZZA

So attractive. Nice blend of flavors.

Pizza crust dough, your choice, pages 115 to 130 (or partially baked commercial)	1	1
Water	2 cups	500 mL
Small onion, thinly sliced and separated into rings	1	1
Grated carrot	½ cup	125 mL
Finely chopped celery	¼ cup	60 mL
Bay leaf	1	1
Golden raisins	¼ cup	60 mL
Ground thyme, just a pinch		
Brown sugar, packed	2 tbsp.	30 mL
Lemon juice	2 tbsp.	30 mL
Skinless salmon fillet, diced	½ lb.	225 g
Chili sauce (or ketchup)	¼ cup	60 mL
Grated part-skim mozzarella cheese	1 cup	250 mL
Grated part-skim mozzarella cheese	½ cup	125 mL

Prepare pizza dough. Roll out and press in greased 12 inch (30 cm) pizza pan, forming rim around edge.

Measure next 9 ingredients into medium saucepan. Stir together. Simmer for 15 minutes. Do not drain.

Add salmon. Stir together. Cook for about 4 minutes. Drain well. Discard bay leaf.

Spread chili sauce over crust. Sprinkle with first amount of cheese. Spoon salmon mixture over cheese. Top with second amount of cheese. Bake on bottom rack in 425°F (220°C) oven for about 15 minutes, or for 8 to 10 minutes if using partially baked crust. Cuts into 8 wedges.

1 wedge: 306 Calories; 10.5 g Total Fat; 335 mg Sodium; 15 g Protein; 37 g Carbohydrate; 2 g Dietary Fiber

Pictured on page 125.

SHRIMP CREOLE PIZZA

You may want to make this more southern yet by adding more cayenne pepper.

Rice Pizza Crust, page 122 (or other)	1	1
Cooking oil	2 tsp.	10 mL
Chopped onion	½ cup	125 mL
Chopped celery	¼ cup	60 mL
Medium green pepper, cut into 2 inch (5 cm) slivers	½	½
Canned tomatoes, drained, diced and drained again	14 oz.	398 mL
Ketchup	2 tbsp.	30 mL
Chili powder	1 tsp.	5 mL
Salt	½ tsp.	2 mL
Pepper	⅛ tsp.	0.5 mL
Cayenne pepper	⅛ tsp.	0.5 mL
Cooked small or medium fresh (or frozen, thawed) shrimp	½ lb.	225 g
Grated part-skim mozzarella cheese	¾ cup	175 mL

Prepare rice crust but do not bake.

Heat cooking oil in medium frying pan. Add onion, celery and green pepper. Sauté until vegetables are soft but not browned.

Add next 6 ingredients. Stir together. Spread over rice crust.

Arrange shrimp over top. Cover with cheese. Bake on bottom rack in 425°F (220°C) oven for 15 to 20 minutes. Cuts into 8 wedges.

1 wedge: 227 Calories; 3.9 g Total Fat; 456 mg Sodium; 13 g Protein; 35 g Carbohydrate; 2 g Dietary Fiber

Do you have to be Einstein to make wisecracks?

MAPLE PECAN HALIBUT PIZZA

A very different presentation as well as a surprise. Finished with a drizzle of syrup and nuts. Try for an appetizer by simply cutting into smaller wedges.

Pizza crust dough, your choice, pages 115 to 130 (or partially baked commercial)	1	1
Cooking oil	1 tsp.	5 mL
Chopped onion	1 cup	250 mL
Cooking oil	1 tsp.	5 mL
Halibut steak (or other firm flesh fish)	¾ lb.	340 g
Corn syrup	¼ cup	60 mL
Maple flavoring	⅛ tsp.	0.5 mL
Salt	⅛ tsp.	0.5 mL
Pepper	¹⁄₁₆ tsp.	0.5 mL
Grated part-skim mozzarella cheese	¾ cup	175 mL
Grated part-skim mozzarella cheese	¾ cup	175 mL
Ground pecans	⅓ cup	75 mL

Prepare pizza dough. Roll out and press in greased 12 inch (30 cm) pizza pan, forming rim around edge.

Heat first amount of cooking oil in medium frying pan. Add onion. Sauté until soft. Remove to small bowl.

Add second amount of cooking oil and fish to frying pan. Cook fish on both sides. Cool enough to handle. Remove fish in pieces from bones to bowl with onion.

Stir corn syrup, maple flavoring, salt and pepper together in small cup.

Sprinkle first amount of cheese over crust. Scatter onion and fish over cheese. Sprinkle second amount of cheese over fish. Sprinkle pecans over top. Bake on bottom rack in 425°F (220°C) oven for about 15 minutes, or for 10 minutes if using partially baked crust. Cuts into 8 wedges.

1 wedge: 335 Calories; 12.4 g Total Fat; 268 mg Sodium; 19 g Protein; 37 g Carbohydrate; 2 g Dietary Fiber

From the Malden Hills in Britain. Not the usual tomato flavor.

Pizza crust dough, your choice, pages 115 to 130 (or partially baked commercial)	1	1
All-purpose flour	1 tbsp.	15 mL
Grated Parmesan cheese	2 tbsp.	30 mL
Salt	1/8 tsp.	0.5 mL
Pepper	1/16 tsp.	0.5 mL
Skim evaporated milk	1/2 cup	125 mL
Grated part-skim mozzarella cheese	3/4 cup	175 mL
Canned flaked tuna, drained and broken up	6 1/2 oz.	185 g
Canned small or medium shrimp, drained (or 3/4 cup, 175 mL, frozen, cooked)	4 oz.	113 g
Fresh (or frozen) kernel corn	1/2 cup	125 mL
Grated part-skim mozzarella cheese	3/4 cup	175 mL

Prepare pizza dough. Roll out and press in greased 12 inch (30 cm) pizza pan, forming rim around edge.

Measure next 4 ingredients into small saucepan. Gradually whisk in evaporated milk. Heat and stir until mixture is boiling and thickened. Place saucepan in cold water. Stir to cool. Spread over crust.

Layer remaining 5 ingredients over top in order given. Bake on bottom rack in 425°F (220°C) oven for 13 to 15 minutes, or for 8 minutes if using partially baked crust. Cuts into 8 wedges.

1 wedge: 285 Calories; 8.7 g Total Fat; 383 mg Sodium; 20 g Protein; 31 g Carbohydrate; 1 g Dietary Fiber

Do you take a sick bird to get a tweetment?

GARDEN PIZZA

Sun-dried tomatoes and green vegetables add color. The crust adds wonderful flavor.

Confetti Biscuit Pizza Crust dough, page 130 (or other biscuit crust)	1	1
Sun-dried tomatoes	¹/₂ cup	125 mL
Boiling water, to cover		
Chopped onion	1 cup	250 mL
Hard margarine (or butter)	2 tsp.	10 mL
Basic Pizza Sauce, page 132 (or other)	¹/₂ cup	125 mL
Grated part-skim mozzarella cheese	³/₄ cup	175 mL
Frozen chopped spinach, thawed and squeezed dry	¹/₂ x 10 oz.	¹/₂ x 300 g
Chopped cooked broccoli	¹/₂ cup	125 mL
Sliced fresh mushrooms	1 cup	250 mL
Grated part-skim mozzarella cheese	³/₄ cup	175 mL

Prepare pizza dough. Roll out and press in greased 12 inch (30 cm) pizza pan, forming rim around edge.

Cover tomatoes with boiling water in small bowl. Let soak for 25 minutes. Drain. Cut into 4 or 5 pieces each.

Sauté onion in margarine in medium frying pan until soft.

Spread sauce over crust. Sprinkle with first amount of cheese. Layer tomatoes, onion, spinach, broccoli and mushrooms over cheese. Scatter second amount of cheese over top. Bake on bottom rack in 425°F (220°C) oven for about 15 minutes. Cuts into 8 wedges.

1 wedge: 299 Calories; 12.9 g Total Fat; 396 mg Sodium; 11 g Protein; 35 g Carbohydrate; 3 g Dietary Fiber

Pictured on page 143.

Dracula's favorite ship is a blood vessel.

In honor of Queen Margherita of Italy. Note the colors of the Italian flag—red, white and green. Very good.

Basic Pizza Crust dough, page 115 (or other)	1	1
Plum tomatoes, peeled, seeded and chopped (or 1 can, 14 oz., 398 mL, Italian, drained and chopped)	1 lb.	454 g
Granulated sugar (optional)	¹/₂ tsp.	2 mL
Ground thyme	¹/₈ tsp.	0.5 mL
Salt	¹/₂ tsp.	2 mL
Pepper	¹/₈ tsp.	0.5 mL
Grated mozzarella cheese	³/₄ cup	175 mL
Grated Edam cheese	³/₄ cup	175 mL
Grated Parmesan cheese	2 tbsp.	30 mL
Grated Parmesan cheese	1 tbsp.	15 mL
Chopped fresh sweet basil (see Note)	¹/₂ cup	125 mL

Prepare pizza dough. Roll out and press in greased 12 inch (30 cm) pizza pan, forming rim around edge.

Scatter tomato over crust.

Mix sugar, thyme, salt and pepper in small cup. Sprinkle over tomato.

Sprinkle mozzarella cheese, Edam cheese and first amount of Parmesan cheese over top. Bake on bottom rack in 425°F (220°C) oven for about 15 minutes, or for about 8 minutes if using partially baked crust.

Sprinkle with second amount of Parmesan cheese and basil. Cuts into 8 wedges.

Note: Fresh basil looks better than dried, but if you only have dried basil, sprinkle 1 tbsp. (15 mL) over top when removed from oven.

1 wedge: 245 Calories; 9.6 g Total Fat; 465 mg Sodium; 11 g Protein; 29 g Carbohydrate; 2 g Dietary Fiber

FIVE CHEESE PIZZA

Cheesy of course!

Pizza crust dough, your choice, pages 115 to 130 (or partially baked commercial)	1	1
Garden Tomato Pizza Sauce, page 136 (or other)	½ cup	125 mL
Grated part-skim mozzarella cheese	¾ cup	175 mL
Grated fontina cheese	½ cup	125 mL
Grated provolone cheese	1 cup	250 mL
Grated Romano (or Parmesan) cheese	3 tbsp.	50 mL
Ricotta cheese (or dry curd cottage cheese)	½ cup	125 mL
Grated part-skim mozzarella cheese	½ cup	125 mL
Chopped fresh parsley (or 1 tsp., 5 mL, flakes)	1½ tbsp.	25 mL
Chopped green onion	2 tbsp.	30 mL

Prepare pizza dough. Roll out and press in greased 12 inch (30 cm) pizza pan, forming rim around edge.

Spread sauce over crust.

Add next 6 ingredients in layers in order given.

Sprinkle with parsley and green onion. Bake on bottom rack in 425°F (220°C) oven for 13 to 15 minutes, or for about 8 minutes if using partially baked crust. Cuts into 8 wedges.

1 wedge: 324 Calories; 15.4 g Total Fat; 450 mg Sodium; 17 g Protein; 29 g Carbohydrate; 2 g Dietary Fiber

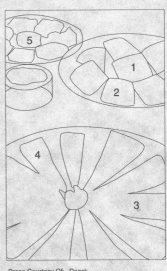

1. Taco Pizza Squares, page 15 (on Cornmeal Pizza Crust)
2. Mexi-Appies, page 20
3. Nacho Pizza, page 24
4. Guacamole Pizza, page 21
5. Fast Chili Pizza Appetizers, page 22

Props Courtesy Of: Dansk
The Bay

BROCCOLI MUSHROOM PIZZA

Like tiny trees in a golden pond.

Pizza crust dough, your choice, pages 115 to 130 (or partially baked commercial)	1	1
Frozen chopped broccoli Water, to cover	10 oz.	300 g
Hard margarine (or butter) Chopped onion	2 tsp. 1 cup	10 mL 250 mL
Condensed cream of mushroom soup Canned mushroom pieces, drained Salt Pepper	$\frac{1}{2}$ × 10 oz. 10 oz. $\frac{1}{4}$ tsp. $\frac{1}{8}$ tsp.	$\frac{1}{2}$ × 284 mL 284 mL 1 mL 0.5 mL
Grated medium Cheddar cheese Garlic powder, light sprinkle (optional but good)	1 cup	250 mL

Prepare pizza dough. Roll out and press in greased 12 inch (30 cm) pizza pan, forming rim around edge.

Cook broccoli in water in medium saucepan until tender-crisp. Drain. Put into small bowl.

Melt margarine in medium frying pan. Add onion. Sauté until soft. Add to broccoli.

Stir soup, mushrooms, salt and pepper together in medium bowl. Spread over crust. Spoon broccoli mixture over top.

Sprinkle with cheese and garlic powder. Bake on bottom rack in 425°F (220°C) oven for about 20 minutes, or for about 10 minutes if using partially baked crust. Cuts into 8 wedges.

1 wedge: 262 Calories; 11.3 g Total Fat; 511 mg Sodium; 9 g Protein; 31 g Carbohydrate; 3 g Dietary Fiber

Golddiggers are human gimmee pigs.

DELPHI PIZZA

Lots of veggies in this green and white dish.

Pizza crust dough, your choice, pages 115 to 130 (or partially baked commercial)	1	1
Green pepper, chopped	1	1
Chopped onion	1 cup	250 mL
Chopped fresh mushrooms	1 cup	250 mL
Cooking oil	2 tsp.	10 mL
Broccoli florets	1 cup	250 mL
Water, to cover		
Basic Pizza Sauce, page 132 (or other)	½ cup	125 mL
Frozen spinach, thawed and drained	10 oz.	300 g
Grated part-skim mozzarella cheese	1 cup	250 mL
Crumbled feta cheese	¾ cup	175 mL

Prepare pizza dough. Roll out and press in greased 12 inch (30 cm) pizza pan, forming rim around edge.

Sauté green pepper, onion and mushrooms in cooking oil in medium frying pan until soft.

Cook broccoli in water in small saucepan until tender-crisp. Do not overcook. Drain. Coarsely chop. Add to mushroom mixture.

Spread sauce over crust. Arrange spinach over sauce. Spoon mushroom mixture over top. Sprinkle mozzarella cheese and feta cheese over top. Bake on bottom rack in 425°F (220°C) oven for about 15 minutes, or for 10 minutes if using partially baked crust. Cuts into 8 wedges.

1 wedge: 267 Calories; 10.7 g Total Fat; 321 mg Sodium; 11 g Protein; 32 g Carbohydrate; 3 g Dietary Fiber

He lives like a cafeteria—self service only.

Lots of vegetables in this ra-tuh-TOO-ee pizza with Italian flavoring.

Pizza crust dough, your choice, pages 115 to 130 (or partially baked commercial)	1	1
Cooking oil	1½ tbsp.	25 mL
Dried sweet basil	¼ tsp.	1 mL
Dried whole oregano	¼ tsp.	1 mL
Ground thyme	⅛ tsp.	0.5 mL
Garlic powder	½ tsp.	2 mL
Parsley flakes	1 tsp.	5 mL
Salt	½ tsp.	2 mL
Pepper	⅛ tsp.	0.5 mL
Small narrow eggplant, with peel, diced (about ½ lb., 225 g)	1	1
Small zucchini, with peel, diced (about ½ lb., 225 g)	1	1
Sliced onion	½ cup	125 mL
Medium red pepper, sliced	1	1
Grated part-skim mozzarella cheese	¾ cup	175 mL
Medium tomatoes, diced and patted dry	2	2
Grated part-skim mozzarella cheese	¾ cup	175 mL
Grated Parmesan cheese	2 tbsp.	30 mL

Prepare pizza dough. Roll out and press in greased 12 inch (30 cm) pizza pan, forming rim around edge.

Measure next 8 ingredients into large bowl. Stir together.

Add all 4 vegetables. Toss well to coat. Spread on greased baking pan. Bake on top rack in 425°F (220°C) oven for about 15 minutes. Cool for 10 minutes.

Sprinkle crust with first amount of mozzarella cheese. Spoon roasted vegetables over cheese.

Scatter tomato over vegetables. Sprinkle second amount of mozzarella cheese and Parmesan cheese over top. Bake on bottom rack in 425°F (220°C) oven for 15 to 20 minutes, or for 10 to 12 minutes if using partially baked crust. Cuts into 8 wedges.

1 wedge: *269 Calories; 11 g Total Fat; 397 mg Sodium; 11 g Protein; 32 g Carbohydrate; 3 g Dietary Fiber*

TOMATO BROCCOLI PIZZA

Bright and appealing. A refreshing pizza.

Pizza crust dough, your choice, pages 115 to 130 (or partially baked commercial)	1	1
Chopped or sliced onion	½ cup	125 mL
Cooking oil	2 tsp.	10 mL
Broccoli florets (generous measure)	1 cup	250 mL
Water, to cover		
Favorite Tomato Pizza Sauce, page 138 (or other)	½ cup	125 mL
Grated part-skim mozzarella cheese	¾ cup	175 mL
Sliced fresh mushrooms	½ cup	125 mL
Roma tomatoes, seeded and diced	2	2
Grated part-skim mozzarella cheese	¾ cup	175 mL

Prepare pizza dough. Roll out and press in greased 12 inch (30 cm) pizza pan, forming rim around edge.

Sauté onion in cooking oil in small frying pan until soft and golden.

Cook broccoli in water in small saucepan until tender-crisp. Do not overcook. Drain well. Coarsely chop.

Spread sauce over crust. Sprinkle first amount of cheese over sauce. Spread onion over cheese. Scatter broccoli over onion. Sprinkle with mushroom slices. Layer tomato over all. Top with second amount of cheese. Bake on bottom rack in 425°F (220°C) oven for 13 to 15 minutes, or for 10 minutes if using partially baked crust. Cuts into 8 wedges.

1 wedge: 248 Calories; 9 g Total Fat; 315 mg Sodium; 10 g Protein; 32 g Carbohydrate; 2 g Dietary Fiber

Pictured on page 143.

Paré Pointer

He seems to be part animal. Notice his bear feet, the calves on his legs, the frog in his throat and the bull on his tongue.

A satisfying appetizing pizza. Excellent choice. Attractive.

Pizza crust dough, your choice, pages 115 to 130 (or partially baked commercial)	1	1
Chopped red onion	1 cup	250 mL
Cooking oil	1 tsp.	5 mL
Broccoli florets	1 cup	250 mL
Water, to cover		
Basic Pizza Sauce, page 132 (or other)	½ cup	125 mL
Grated part-skim mozzarella cheese	¾ cup	175 mL
Canned artichoke hearts, drained and chopped	14 oz.	398 mL
Salt, sprinkle		
Pepper, sprinkle		
Grated part-skim mozzarella cheese	¾ cup	175 mL

Prepare pizza dough. Roll out and press in greased 12 inch (30 cm) pizza pan, forming rim around edge.

Sauté red onion in cooking oil in medium frying pan for about 3 minutes until soft.

Cook broccoli in water in small saucepan until tender-crisp. Drain. Coarsely chop.

Spread sauce over crust. Sprinkle with first amount of cheese. Scatter red onion, artichoke, broccoli, salt and pepper in layers over sauce. Sprinkle second amount of cheese over top. Bake on bottom rack in 425°F (220°C) oven for about 15 minutes, or for 8 minutes if using partially baked crust. Cuts into 8 wedges.

1 wedge: 248 Calories; 8.3 g Total Fat; 359 mg Sodium; 11 g Protein; 33 g Carbohydrate; 3 g Dietary Fiber

He who has imagination without learning has wings but no feet.

MACARONI PIZZA

Here's a novel way to dress up a box of macaroni and cheese. Colorful, good tasting and different.

MACARONI PIZZA CRUST

Package of macaroni and cheese dinner	7³/₄ oz.	225 g
Large eggs, fork-beaten	2	2

TOPPING

Marinara Pizza Sauce, page 137 (or other)	²/₃ cup	150 mL
Tofu (or regular) wieners, cut into coins	3	3
Canned sliced mushrooms, drained	10 oz.	284 mL
Grated part-skim mozzarella cheese	1¹/₂ cups	375 mL
Grated Parmesan cheese	1 tbsp.	15 mL
Pimiento-stuffed green olives, sliced (optional)	10	10

Macaroni Pizza Crust: Prepare macaroni and cheese dinner according to package directions.

Stir in eggs. Spread in greased 12 inch (30 cm) pizza pan. Bake on bottom rack in 350°F (175°C) oven for 10 minutes.

Topping: Spread sauce over crust to within ¹/₂ inch (12 mm) of edge. Scatter wiener coins over sauce. Sprinkle mushrooms, mozzarella cheese, Parmesan cheese and olive slices over top. Return to oven for about 10 minutes. Cuts into 8 wedges.

1 wedge: 283 Calories; 12.6 g Total Fat; 493 mg Sodium; 19 g Protein; 25 g Carbohydrate; 1 g Dietary Fiber

Pictured on page 143.

He's not feeling like himself lately. Have you noticed the improvement?

A crust that will work for any regular pizza.

All-purpose flour	2 cups	500 mL
Instant yeast	1¼ tsp.	6 mL
Salt	¼ tsp.	1 mL
Warm water	⅔ cup	150 mL
Cooking oil	2 tbsp.	30 mL

Food Processor Method: Put first 3 ingredients into food processor fitted with dough blade.

With machine running, pour warm water and cooking oil through tube in lid. Process for 50 to 60 seconds. If dough seems sticky to remove, add about ½ tsp. (2 mL) flour to make it easier to handle.

Hand Method: Put first 3 ingredients into medium bowl. Stir together well.

Add warm water and cooking oil. Mix well until dough leaves sides of bowl. Knead on lightly floured surface for 5 to 8 minutes until smooth and elastic.

To Complete: At this point you may choose to roll out and press in greased 12 inch (30 cm) pizza pan, forming rim around edge. Or place dough in large greased bowl, turning once to grease top. Cover with tea towel. Let stand in oven with light on and door closed for about 1 hour until doubled in size. Punch dough down. Roll out and press in greased 12 inch (30 cm) pizza pan, forming rim around edge.

*⅛ **crust**: 153 Calories; 3.8 g Total Fat; 86 mg Sodium; 4 g Protein; 25 g Carbohydrate; 1 g Dietary Fiber*

Pictured on front cover and on pages 35, 89, 125 and 143.

TACO PIZZA CRUST: Mix ½ envelope of 1¼ oz. (35 g) taco seasoning mix into dry ingredients before adding wet ingredients.

THIN BASIC PIZZA CRUST: Reduce flour to 1½ cups (375 mL) and reduce water to ½ cup (125 mL). Crust will cook a bit quicker.

CALZONE PIZZA CRUST: Use Basic Pizza Crust or other crust as long as 2 cups (500 mL) flour are used. Makes 4 calzones.

Pictured on page 89.

BASIC DOUBLE PIZZA CRUST

Makes a thin bottom and top crust. Use for any double crust pizza, pages 93 to 96.

All-purpose flour	3 cups	750 mL
Instant yeast	2½ tsp.	12 mL
Granulated sugar	1½ tsp.	7 mL
Salt	½ tsp.	2 mL
Warm water, approximately	⅞ cup	200 mL
Cooking oil	3 tbsp.	50 mL

Food Processor Method: Put first 4 ingredients into food processor fitted with dough blade.

With machine running, pour warm water and cooking oil through tube in lid. Process for 50 to 60 seconds.

Hand Method: Put first 4 ingredients into medium bowl. Stir together.

Add warm water and cooking oil. Mix well until dough leaves sides of bowl. Knead on lightly floured surface for 6 to 8 minutes until smooth and elastic.

To Complete: At this point you may choose to roll out and press in greased 12 inch (30 cm) pizza pan, forming rim around edge. Or place dough in large greased bowl, turning once to grease top. Cover with tea towel. Let stand in oven with light on and door closed for about 1 hour until doubled in size. Punch dough down. Makes 2 crusts to fit 12 inch (30 cm) pizza pan.

⅛ crust: 232 Calories; 5.7 g Total Fat; 171 mg Sodium; 6 g Protein; 39 g Carbohydrate; 2 g Dietary Fiber

CORNMEAL PIZZA CRUST

Cornmeal adds extra flavor and a bit of a crunch.

All-purpose flour	2 cups	500 mL
Yellow cornmeal	⅓ cup	75 mL
Instant yeast	1¼ tsp.	6 mL
Salt	¼ tsp.	1 mL
Fancy molasses	2 tbsp.	30 mL
Warm water	⅞ cup	200 mL
Cooking oil	2 tbsp.	30 mL

Food Processor Method: Put first 4 ingredients into food processor fitted with dough blade.

Stir molasses into warm water in small bowl. With machine running, pour molasses-water mixture and cooking oil through tube in lid. Process for 50 to 60 seconds. If dough seems sticky to remove, add about ½ tsp. (2 mL) flour to make it easier to handle.

(continued on next page)

Hand Method: Put first 4 ingredients into medium bowl. Stir together.

Add warm water, molasses and cooking oil to flour mixture. Mix well until dough leaves sides of bowl. Knead on lightly floured surface for 5 to 8 minutes until smooth and elastic.

To Complete: At this point you may choose to roll out and press in greased 12 inch (30 cm) pizza pan, forming rim around edge. Or place dough in large greased bowl, turning once to grease top. Cover with tea towel. Let stand in oven with light on and door closed for about 1 hour until doubled in size. Punch dough down. Roll out and press in greased 12 inch (30 cm) pizza pan, forming rim around edge.

⅛ crust: 188 Calories; 3.9 g Total Fat; 87 mg Sodium; 4 g Protein; 34 g Carbohydrate; 1 g Dietary Fiber

Pictured on page 107.

WHOLE WHEAT PIZZA CRUST

So easy to make crusts healthier.

Whole wheat flour	1 cup	250 mL
All-purpose flour	1 cup	250 mL
Granulated sugar	½ tsp.	2 mL
Salt	¼ tsp.	1 mL
Instant yeast	1¼ tsp.	6 mL
Warm water	¾ cup	175 mL
Cooking oil	2 tbsp.	30 mL

Food Processor Method: Put first 5 ingredients into food processor fitted with dough blade.

With machine running, pour warm water and cooking oil through tube in lid. Process for 50 to 60 seconds. If dough seems sticky to remove, add about ½ tsp. (2 mL) flour to make it easier to handle.

Hand Method: Put first 5 ingredients into medium bowl. Stir together well.

Add warm water and cooking oil. Mix well until dough leaves sides of bowl. Knead on lightly floured surface for 5 to 8 minutes until smooth and elastic.

To Complete: At this point you may choose to roll out and press in greased 12 inch (30 cm) pizza pan, forming rim around edge. Or place dough in large greased bowl, turning once to grease top. Cover with tea towel. Let stand in oven with light on and door closed for about 1 hour until doubled in size. Punch dough down. Roll out and press in greased 12 inch (30 cm) pizza pan, forming rim around edge.

⅛ crust: 147 Calories; 3.9 g Total Fat; 86 mg Sodium; 4 g Protein; 25 g Carbohydrate; 3 g Dietary Fiber

PUMPERNICKEL PIZZA CRUST

Great flavor. No one will leave their crust on this one.

All-purpose flour	1 cup	250 mL
Rye flour (dark or light)	¾ cup	175 mL
Cocoa	4 tsp.	20 mL
Instant yeast	2½ tsp.	12 mL
Granulated sugar	2 tsp.	10 mL
Caraway seed (optional)	2 tsp.	10 mL
Salt	½ tsp.	2 mL
Fancy molasses	1½ tbsp.	25 mL
Warm water	⅔ cup	150 mL
Cooking oil	2 tbsp.	30 mL

Food Processor Method: Put first 7 ingredients into food processor fitted with dough blade.

Stir molasses into warm water in small bowl. With machine running, pour molasses-water mixture and cooking oil through tube in lid. Process for 50 to 60 seconds. If dough seems sticky to remove, add about ½ tsp. (2 mL) flour to make it easier to handle.

Hand Method: Put first 7 ingredients into medium bowl. Stir together well.

Add warm water, molasses and cooking oil. Mix well until dough leaves sides of bowl. Knead on lightly floured surface for 5 to 8 minutes until smooth and elastic.

To Complete: At this point you may choose to roll out and press in greased 12 inch (30 cm) pizza pan, forming rim around edge. Or place dough in large greased bowl, turning once to grease top. Cover with tea towel. Let stand in oven with light on and door closed for about 1 hour until doubled in size. Punch dough down. Roll out and press in greased 12 inch (30 cm) pizza pan, forming rim around edge.

⅛ *crust: 147 Calories; 3.9 g Total Fat; 172 mg Sodium; 3 g Protein; 25 g Carbohydrate; 3 g Dietary Fiber*

Pictured on page 17.

TOMATO HERB PIZZA CRUST

Reddish-orange in color with a good mix of spices.

All-purpose flour	2 cups	500 mL
Instant yeast	1¼ tsp.	6 mL
Dried sweet basil	2 tsp.	10 mL
Dried whole oregano	¼ tsp.	1 mL
Garlic powder	¼ tsp.	1 mL
Salt	¼ tsp.	1 mL
Pepper	⅛ tsp.	0.5 mL
Granulated sugar	1 tsp.	5 mL
Warm tomato juice	¾ cup	175 mL
Cooking oil	2 tbsp.	30 mL

Food Processor Method: Put first 8 ingredients into food processor fitted with dough blade.

With machine running, pour tomato juice and cooking oil through tube in lid. Process for 50 to 60 seconds. If dough seems sticky to remove, add about ½ tsp. (2 mL) flour to make it easier to handle.

Hand Method: Put first 8 ingredients into medium bowl. Stir together.

Add tomato juice and cooking oil. Mix well until dough leaves sides of bowl. Knead on lightly floured surface for 5 to 8 minutes until smooth and elastic.

To Complete: At this point you may choose to roll out and press in greased 12 inch (30 cm) pizza pan, forming rim around edge. Or place dough in large greased bowl, turning once to grease top. Cover with tea towel. Let stand in oven with light on and door closed for about 1 hour until doubled in size. Punch dough down. Roll out and press in greased 12 inch (30 cm) pizza pan, forming rim around edge.

⅛ *crust: 185 Calories; 3.9 g Total Fat; 408 mg Sodium; 4 g Protein; 34 g Carbohydrate; 2 g Dietary Fiber*

Paré Pointer

How come giraffes don't get sore throats when they get wet feet? They do but not until the following week.

FOCACCIA PIZZA CRUST

This lends itself to be eaten as bread as well as with toppings.

All-purpose flour	2 cups	500 mL
Instant yeast	1½ tsp.	7 mL
Granulated sugar	½ tsp.	2 mL
Salt	¼ tsp.	1 mL
Warm water	⅔ cup	150 mL
Olive (or cooking) oil	2 tsp.	10 mL
Olive (or cooking) oil	4 tsp.	20 mL
Ground rosemary	½ tsp.	2 mL
Ground thyme	¼ tsp.	1 mL
Ground oregano	⅛ tsp.	0.5 mL
Dill weed	⅛ tsp.	0.5 mL

Coarse sea salt, sprinkle

Food Processor Method: Put first 4 ingredients into food processor fitted with dough blade.

With machine running, pour warm water and olive oil through tube in lid. Process for 50 to 60 seconds.

Hand Method: Put first 4 ingredients into medium bowl. Stir together.

Add warm water and olive oil. Mix well until dough leaves sides of bowl. Knead on lightly floured surface for 6 to 8 minutes until smooth and elastic.

To Complete: Place dough in large greased bowl, turning once to grease top. Cover with tea towel. Let stand in oven with light on and door closed for about 1 hour until doubled in size. Roll out and stretch to fit greased 12 inch (30 cm) pizza pan, forming rim around edge. Let rise in oven once more for about 30 minutes.

Press all over surface, making dents with your fingertips. Drizzle olive oil over top allowing it to pool in dents.

Stir rosemary, thyme, oregano and dill weed together in small cup. Sprinkle over top.

Sprinkle with sea salt. Bake on bottom rack in 400°F (205°C) oven for about 20 minutes.

⅛ crust: 154 Calories; 3.8 g Total Fat; 86 mg Sodium; 4 g Protein; 26 g Carbohydrate; 1 g Dietary Fiber

Pictured on page 35.

Pronounced bree-AHSH. A richer and softer crust than most.

All-purpose flour	2 cups	500 mL
Instant yeast	1¼ tsp.	6 mL
Granulated sugar	1 tbsp.	15 mL
Salt	¼ tsp.	1 mL
Warm milk	¼ cup	60 mL
Large eggs, fork-beaten	2	2
Hard margarine (or butter), melted and cooled to luke warm	3 tbsp.	50 mL

Food Processor Method: Put first 4 ingredients into food processor fitted with dough blade.

With machine running, pour remaining 3 ingredients through tube in lid. Process for 50 to 60 seconds. If dough seems sticky to remove, add about ½ tsp. (2 mL) flour to make it easier to handle.

Hand Method: Put first 4 ingredients into medium bowl. Stir together well.

Add warm milk, eggs and melted margarine. Mix well until dough leaves sides of bowl. Knead on lightly floured surface for 5 to 8 minutes until smooth and elastic.

To Complete: At this point you may choose to roll out and press in greased 12 inch (30 cm) pizza pan, forming rim around edge. Or place dough in large greased bowl, turning once to grease top. Cover with tea towel. Let stand in oven with light on and door closed for about 1 hour until doubled in size. Punch dough down. Roll out and press in greased 12 inch (30 cm) pizza pan, forming rim around edge.

⅛ *crust: 186 Calories; 5.7 g Total Fat; 153 mg Sodium; 6 g Protein; 28 g Carbohydrate; 1 g Dietary Fiber*

Pictured on page 125.

Paré Pointer

Husband working on taxes, to wife: "Let me explain it this way, Dear. We have six apples. The IRS wants seven."

RICE PIZZA CRUST

Ideal for Curried Chicken Pizza, page 65, Jambalaya Pizza, page 97, or Shrimp Creole Pizza, page 101.

Long grain rice	½ cup	125 mL
Boiling water	1 cup	250 mL
All-purpose flour	1½ cups	375 mL
Instant yeast	1¼ tsp.	6 mL
Warm water	½ cup	125 mL

Cook rice in boiling water in small covered saucepan for about 15 minutes until rice is tender and water is absorbed. Measure 1¼ cups (300 mL) and empty into medium bowl. Cool to lukewarm.

Add flour and yeast. Stir together well.

Add warm water. Stir together. Turn out onto lightly floured surface. Knead 25 times adding a touch more flour if too sticky. Roll out and press in greased 12 inch (30 cm) pizza pan, forming rim around edge.

⅛ crust: 137 Calories; 0.3 g Total Fat; 1 mg Sodium; 4 g Protein; 29 g Carbohydrate; 1 g Dietary Fiber

BROWN RICE CRUST: Omit white rice and use brown rice. Cook in boiling water for 35 to 45 minutes until rice is tender and water is absorbed.

JUMBO PIZZA CRUST

An old-fashioned medium-thick crust. Excellent choice. Enough dough to fit a jelly roll pan.

Granulated sugar	1 tsp.	5 mL
Warm water	1 cup	250 mL
Envelope active dry yeast (1 scant tbsp., 15 mL)	1 x ¼ oz.	1 x 8 g
All-purpose flour	2¾ cups	675 mL
Salt	½ tsp.	2 mL
Cooking oil	2 tbsp.	30 mL

Stir sugar into warm water in small bowl. Sprinkle with yeast. Let stand for 10 minutes. Stir together to dissolve yeast.

(continued on next page)

Add flour, salt and cooking oil. Mix well until dough leaves sides of bowl. Knead dough on lightly floured surface 100 times. Place dough in large greased bowl, turning once to grease top. Cover with tea towel. Let stand in oven with light on and door closed for about 1 hour until doubled in size. Punch dough down. Roll out and press in greased 10 x 15 inch (25 x 38 cm) jelly roll pan.

1/12 crust: 133 Calories; 2.6 g Total Fat; 114 mg Sodium; 3 g Protein; 24 g Carbohydrate; 1 g Dietary Fiber

DILL PIZZA CRUST

Especially good for fish and seafood pizzas.

All-purpose flour	2 cups	500 mL
Instant yeast	1½ tsp.	7 mL
Granulated sugar	1½ tsp.	7 mL
Dill weed	1½ tsp.	7 mL
Onion powder	½ tsp.	2 mL
Parsley flakes	½ tsp.	2 mL
Salt	¼ tsp.	1 mL
Creamed cottage cheese, warmed	⅔ cup	150 mL
Large egg	1	1
Cooking oil	2 tbsp.	30 mL

Food Processor Method: Put first 7 ingredients into food processor fitted with dough blade.

With machine running, pour remaining 3 ingredients through tube in lid. Process for 50 to 60 seconds. If dough seems sticky to remove, add about ½ tsp. (2 mL) flour to make it easier to handle.

Hand Method: Put first 7 ingredients into medium bowl. Stir together well.

Add cottage cheese, egg and cooking oil. Mix well until dough leaves sides of bowl. Knead on lightly floured surface for 5 to 8 minutes until smooth and elastic.

To Complete: At this point you may choose to roll out and press in greased 12 inch (30 cm) pizza pan, forming rim around edge. Or place dough in large greased bowl, turning once to grease top. Cover with tea towel. Let stand in oven with light on and door closed for about 1 hour until doubled in size. Punch dough down. Roll out and press in 12 inch (30 cm) pizza pan, forming rim around edge.

1/8 crust: 181 Calories; 4.6 g Total Fat; 178 mg Sodium; 7 g Protein; 27 g Carbohydrate; 1 g Dietary Fiber

RYE PIZZA CRUST

This crust is perfect for Reuben Pizza, page 31.

All-purpose flour	1 cup	250 mL
Rye flour (dark or light)	1 cup	250 mL
Granulated sugar	1 tsp.	5 mL
Salt	1/4 tsp.	1 mL
Instant yeast	2 1/2 tsp.	12 mL
Fancy molasses	2 tbsp.	30 mL
Warm water	2/3 cup	150 mL
Cooking oil	2 tbsp.	30 mL

Food Processor Method: Put first 5 ingredients into food processor fitted with dough blade.

Stir molasses into warm water in small bowl. With machine running, pour molasses-water mixture and cooking oil through tube in lid. Process for 50 to 60 seconds.

Hand Method: Put first 5 ingredients into medium bowl. Stir together well.

Add warm water, molasses and cooking oil. Mix well until dough leaves sides of bowl. Knead on lightly floured surface for 6 to 8 minutes until smooth and elastic.

To Complete: At this point you may choose to roll out and press in greased 12 inch (30 cm) pizza pan, forming rim around edge. Or place dough in large greased bowl, turning once to grease top. Cover with tea towel. Let stand in oven with light on and door closed for about 1 hour until doubled in size. Punch dough down. Roll out and press in greased 12 inch (30 cm) pizza pan, forming rim around edge.

1/8 crust: 157 Calories; 3.9 g Total Fat; 87 mg Sodium; 3 g Protein; 27 g Carbohydrate; 3 g Dietary Fiber

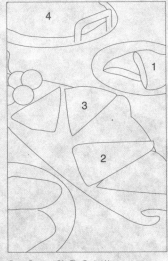

1. Seafood Calzones, page 46
2. Festive Salmon Pizza, page 100
3. Shrimp And Mushroom Pizza, page 99
   (on Basic Pizza Crust)
4. Crab Louis Salad Pizza, page 150
   (on Brioche Pizza Crust)

Props Courtesy Of: The Basket House
The Bay

SOURDOUGH STARTER

Use this starter for making Sourdough Pizza Crust, below. Mixture will keep up to one month without replenishing, or use and replenish for several years.

Granulated sugar	2 tsp.	10 mL
Warm water	2 cups	500 mL
Envelope active dry yeast (1 scant tbsp., 15 mL)	1 x ¼ oz.	1 x 8 g
All-purpose flour	2 cups	500 mL
Salt	½ tsp.	2 mL

Stir sugar into warm water in medium bowl. Sprinkle yeast over top. Let stand for 10 minutes. Stir together to dissolve yeast.

Add flour and salt. Mix well. Pour into large ice cream pail or other 4 quart (4 L) container. Do not use metal container. Cover top with 3 layers of cheesecloth. Let stand at room temperature for 3 to 5 days. Stir 2 or 3 times each day. Mixture will "grow" in volume and look bubbly the first day, then settle down. The mixture will also separate but stirring will bring it together. Starter is ready when it has a "sour," not yeasty, smell. Mixture may now be kept in 2 quart (2 L) jar or other plastic container. Cover and refrigerate.

To Replenish Starter: For each ¾ cup (175 mL) starter used, add ¾ cup (175 mL) each, of flour and water and 1 tsp. (5 mL) sugar. Mix well. Cover. Let stand at room temperature until bubbly. Refrigerate.

SOURDOUGH PIZZA CRUST

Nice and light with a yeast flavor. Makes a fairly thin crust. No rising required.

Sourdough Starter, above, room temperature	¾ cup	175 mL
Cooking oil	2 tbsp.	30 mL
All-purpose flour	1 cup	250 mL
Baking powder	1 tsp.	5 mL
Baking soda	¼ tsp.	1 mL
Salt	¼ tsp.	1 mL

Mix all 6 ingredients in medium bowl. Roll out onto lightly floured surface. Press in greased 12 inch (30 cm) pizza pan, forming rim around edge. Add toppings of your choice. Bake on bottom rack in 425°F (220°C) oven for about 15 minutes. Cuts into 8 wedges.

*⅛ **crust:** 134 Calories; 3.7 g Total Fat; 188 mg Sodium; 3 g Protein; 22 g Carbohydrate; 1 g Dietary Fiber*

BISCUIT PIZZA CRUST

Quicker to prepare than a yeast crust.

All-purpose flour	2 cups	500 mL
Baking powder	1 tbsp.	15 mL
Salt	1/4 tsp.	1 mL
Water	2/3 cup	150 mL
Cooking oil	1 tbsp.	15 mL

Stir flour, baking powder and salt together in medium bowl.

Add water and cooking oil. Stir to form soft ball. Knead on lightly floured surface 8 to 10 times. Roll out and press in greased 12 inch (30 cm) pizza pan, forming rim around edge.

1/8 crust: 138 Calories; 2.1 g Total Fat; 92 mg Sodium; 3 g Protein; 26 g Carbohydrate; 1 g Dietary Fiber

Pictured on front cover and on pages 17, 35, 71 and 89.

THIN BISCUIT PIZZA CRUST: Reduce flour to 1½ cups (375 mL). Reduce water to ½ cup (125 mL). Crust will cook a bit quicker.

WHEAT BISCUIT PIZZA CRUST: Use whole wheat flour for half of all-purpose flour called for.

Pictured on page 143.

DOUBLE BISCUIT PIZZA CRUST

Especially good for Tourtiere Pizza, page 96. Softer than regular crusts.

All-purpose flour	3 cups	750 mL
Baking powder	2 tbsp.	30 mL
Granulated sugar	1 tbsp.	15 mL
Salt	3/4 tsp.	4 mL
Cooking oil	1/3 cup	75 mL
Milk	7/8 cup	200 mL

Stir first 4 ingredients together in medium bowl.

Add cooking oil and milk. Stir together to form soft ball. Knead on lightly floured surface 8 times. Makes 2 crusts to fit 12 inch (30 cm) pizza pan.

1/8 crust: 288 Calories; 10.3 g Total Fat; 282 mg Sodium; 6 g Protein; 42 g Carbohydrate; 2 g Dietary Fiber

BISCUIT MIX PIZZA CRUST

No crust is faster and easier.

Biscuit mix	2 cups	500 mL
Milk, scant measure, approximately	½ cup	125 mL

Measure biscuit mix into medium bowl. Add a bit less milk at first, stirring to form soft ball. If too dry, add a bit more. Turn out onto lightly floured surface. Roll out and press in greased 12 inch (30 cm) pizza pan, forming rim around edge.

⅛ crust: 150 Calories; 4.4 g Total Fat; 448 mg Sodium; 3 g Protein; 24 g Carbohydrate; 1 g Dietary Fiber

SPINACH BISCUIT PIZZA CRUST

Different and colorful. Makes a great foundation for Cheese Bake Pizza, page 22.

Biscuit mix	2 cups	500 mL
Frozen chopped spinach, thawed and squeezed dry	10 oz.	300 g
Large egg	1	1
Milk	⅓ cup	75 mL

Mix all 4 ingredients well in medium bowl to form soft ball. Knead on lightly floured surface 8 times. Roll out and press in greased 12 inch (30 cm) pizza pan, forming rim around edge if desired.

⅛ crust: 162 Calories; 5.1 g Total Fat; 468 mg Sodium; 4 g Protein; 25 g Carbohydrate; 1 g Dietary Fiber

Pictured on page 17.

Paré Pointer

If an axe falls on your car you can be sure you've had an ax-ident.

CONFETTI BISCUIT PIZZA CRUST

Adds interest to any pizza with red and green flecks peeking out.

All-purpose flour	2 cups	500 mL
Baking powder	4 tsp.	20 mL
Granulated sugar	2 tsp.	10 mL
Salt	½ tsp.	2 mL
Chopped green pepper	¼ cup	60 mL
Chopped red pepper	¼ cup	60 mL
Chopped green onion	¼ cup	60 mL
Parsley flakes	1 tsp.	5 mL
Cooking oil	¼ cup	60 mL
Milk	½ cup	125 mL

Measure first 8 ingredients into medium bowl. Mix well.

Add cooking oil and milk. Stir together to form soft ball. Knead on lightly floured surface 8 times. Roll out and press in greased 12 inch (30 cm) pizza pan, forming rim around edge.

⅛ *crust: 202 Calories; 7.8 g Total Fat; 188 mg Sodium; 4 g Protein; 29 g Carbohydrate; 1 g Dietary Fiber*

Pictured on front cover and on page 143.

CHEESY BISCUIT PIZZA CRUST

Cheese is noticeable in the rim of the baked crust. Makes a nice change.

All-purpose flour	2 cups	500 mL
Baking powder	4 tsp.	20 mL
Granulated sugar	4 tsp.	20 mL
Salt	½ tsp.	2 mL
Hard margarine (or butter)	6 tbsp.	100 mL
Milk	¾ cup	175 mL
Grated sharp Cheddar cheese	¾ cup	175 mL

Measure first 5 ingredients into medium bowl. Cut in margarine until crumbly.

Add milk and cheese. Stir together to form soft ball. Knead on lightly floured surface 8 times. Roll out and press in greased 12 inch (30 cm) pizza pan, forming rim around edge.

⅛ *crust: 265 Calories; 13.1 g Total Fat; 364 mg Sodium; 7 g Protein; 29 g Carbohydrate; 1 g Dietary Fiber*

ALL-IN-ONE PIZZA TOPPING

Never run out of toppings. Make multiple recipes and divide and freeze. A quick thaw in the microwave, place on your favorite crust and bake!

Hard margarine (or butter)	**1 tsp.**	**5 mL**
Chopped onion	**½ cup**	**125 mL**
Chopped fresh mushrooms	**¾ cup**	**175 mL**
Grated part-skim mozzarella cheese	**1½ cups**	**375 mL**
Green pepper, slivered or diced	**½**	**1/2**
Red pepper, slivered or diced	**½**	**1/2**
Basic Pizza Sauce, page 132 (or other)	**½ cup**	**125 mL**
Salt, sprinkle		
Pepper, sprinkle		

Select One Of The Following:

Canned broken shrimp, drained	**4 oz.**	**113 g**
Lean ground beef, scramble-fried	**½ lb.**	**225 g**
and drained		
Chopped pepperoni	**½ lb.**	**225 g**
Sausage meat, scramble-fried	**½ lb.**	**225 g**
and drained		

Melt margarine in small frying pan. Add onion. Sauté until soft.

Combine next 7 ingredients in medium bowl. Add onion. Stir together well.

Add your choice of shrimp or meat. Stir together. Freeze in covered container. Makes enough to top 12 inch (30 cm) crust.

⅛ recipe: 94 Calories; 4.6 g Total Fat; 209 mg Sodium; 9 g Protein; 4 g Carbohydrate; 1 g Dietary Fiber

If ostriches didn't have such long legs, how would their feet touch the ground?

BASIC PIZZA SAUCE

Make your own for a real treat. Freezes well.

Cooking oil	2 tsp.	10 mL
Finely chopped onion	1½ cups	375 mL
Garlic cloves, minced (or ¼-½ tsp., 1-2 mL, garlic powder)	1-2	1-2
Canned tomatoes, with juice, broken up	3 × 19 oz.	3 × 540 mL
Finely chopped celery	⅓ cup	75 mL
Ketchup	2 tbsp.	30 mL
Granulated sugar	½ tsp.	2 mL
Bay leaves	2	2
Ground allspice	¼ tsp.	1 mL
Dried sweet basil	1 tsp.	5 mL
Dried whole oregano	1 tsp.	5 mL
Salt	1 tsp.	5 mL
Pepper	¼ tsp.	1 mL

Heat cooking oil in medium saucepan. Add onion and garlic. Sauté until soft.

Add remaining 10 ingredients. Stir together. Heat for about 30 minutes, stirring occasionally, until thickened. Discard bay leaves. Makes 6 cups (1.5 L).

½ cup (125 mL): 61 Calories; 1.3 g Total Fat; 593 mg Sodium; 2 g Protein; 12 g Carbohydrate; 3 g Dietary Fiber

WHITE PIZZA SAUCE

Makes a nice change from tomato sauce on pizzas.

All-purpose flour	⅓ cup	75 mL
Salt	¾ tsp.	4 mL
Pepper	⅛ tsp.	0.5 mL
Paprika	⅛ tsp.	0.5 mL
Onion powder	⅛ tsp.	0.5 mL
Milk	2 cups	500 mL
Hard margarine (or butter), optional	1 tbsp.	15 mL

(continued on next page)

Measure first 5 ingredients into small saucepan. Stir together.

Gradually whisk in milk until no lumps remain. Heat and stir until boiling and thickened.

Stir in margarine until melted. Makes 2 cups (500 mL).

½ cup (125 mL): 95 Calories; 1.5 g Total Fat; 573 mg Sodium; 5 g Protein; 15 g Carbohydrate; trace Dietary Fiber

CHEESE SAUCE: Stir in ½ cup (125 mL) grated medium Cheddar cheese (or more to taste).

SMOKY PIZZA SAUCE

An incredible flavor. Great with wieners, summer sausage or pepperoni. So easy. Freezes well.

Brown sugar, packed	⅔ cup	150 mL
All-purpose flour	2 tbsp.	30 mL
White vinegar	½ cup	125 mL
Lemon juice	2 tbsp.	30 mL
Ketchup	⅓ cup	75 mL
Fancy molasses	¼ cup	60 mL
Prepared mustard	1 tsp.	5 mL
Garlic powder	¼ tsp.	1 mL
Salt	¼ tsp.	1 mL
Liquid smoke	¼ tsp.	1 mL

Stir brown sugar and flour together in small saucepan.

Mix in remaining 8 ingredients. Heat, stirring often, until boiling and thickened. Makes 1½ cups (375 mL).

½ cup (125 mL): 329 Calories; 0.3 g Total Fat; 650 mg Sodium; 1 g Protein; 85 g Carbohydrate; 1 g Dietary Fiber

If you had a flea and a rabbit you would have Bugs Bunny.

RED PEPPER PIZZA SAUCE

Smooth with a delicious flavor.

Medium red peppers, halved	4	4
Chopped onion	½ cup	125 mL
Creamed cottage cheese	¾ cup	175 mL
Water	½ cup	125 mL
All-purpose flour	2 tbsp.	30 mL
Garlic powder	¼ tsp.	1 mL
Salt	¼ tsp.	1 mL
Pepper	⅛ tsp.	0.5 mL
Cayenne pepper	⅛ tsp.	0.5 mL
Chili powder	¼ tsp.	1 mL

Arrange peppers skin side up on broiler pan. Broil about 3 inches (7.5 cm) from heat for 8 to 10 minutes until skins are blackened. Turn over. Broil for about 5 minutes until edges are blackened. Cool enough to handle. Peel off skin. Chop peppers.

Combine pepper with remaining 9 ingredients in blender. Process until smooth. Pour into medium saucepan. Heat for about 10 minutes, stirring often, until boiling and thickened. Makes 2¾ cups (675 mL).

½ cup (125 mL): 56 Calories; 0.5 g Total Fat; 263 mg Sodium; 5 g Protein; 8 g Carbohydrate; 1 g Dietary Fiber

KETCHUP PIZZA SAUCE

When you're out of sauce this saves the day. Easy to assemble. Good anytime. Perfect sauce for Western Pizza, page 43.

Ketchup	½ cup	125 mL
All-purpose flour	1 tbsp.	15 mL
Water	3 tbsp.	50 mL
Prepared mustard	1 tsp.	5 mL
Garlic powder	⅛ tsp.	0.5 mL
Onion powder	⅛ tsp.	0.5 mL
Worcestershire sauce	¼ tsp.	1 mL
Granulated sugar	½ tsp.	2 mL

Measure all 8 ingredients into small saucepan. Whisk until smooth and no lumps of flour remain. Heat, stirring constantly, until boiling and thickened. Makes ⅔ cup (150 mL).

½ cup (125 mL): 148 Calories; 0.7 g Total Fat; 1383 mg Sodium; 3 g Protein; 37 g Carbohydrate; 2 g Dietary Fiber

PICANTE SALSA

A thick, chunky sauce made from ingredients on your shelf. Does not require precooking. Try on Breakfast Pizza, page 41, or Mexican Pizza Con Pollo, page 58.

Tomato paste	5½ oz.	156 mL
Canned chopped green chilies, with liquid	4 oz.	114 mL
Onion flakes	2 tbsp.	30 mL
White vinegar	¼ cup	60 mL
Granulated sugar	1 tbsp.	15 mL
Salt	½ tsp.	2 mL
Garlic powder	¼ tsp.	1 mL
Hot pepper sauce (or more to taste)	½ tsp.	2 mL

Place all 8 ingredients in small bowl. Stir together well. Makes 1½ cups (375 mL).

½ cup (125 mL): 88 Calories; 0.6 g Total Fat; 747 mg Sodium; 3 g Protein; 21 g Carbohydrate; 3 g Dietary Fiber

SPINACH PIZZA SAUCE

This sauce serves as a base for meat or vegetable toppings.

Cooking oil	2 tsp.	10 mL
Chopped onion	1 cup	250 mL
All-purpose flour	2 tbsp.	30 mL
Milk	¾ cup	175 mL
Skim evaporated milk	½ cup	125 mL
Frozen chopped spinach, thawed and squeezed dry	10 oz.	284 mL
Chicken bouillon powder	½ tsp.	2 mL
Salt	¼ tsp.	1 mL
Pepper	⅛ tsp.	0.5 mL
Ground nutmeg, just a pinch		
Grated Parmesan cheese	¼ cup	60 mL

Heat cooking oil in large frying pan. Add onion. Sauté until soft.

Mix in flour. Stir in both milks until boiling and thickened.

Add next 5 ingredients. Heat and stir just until hot.

Stir in cheese. Makes 2 cups (500 mL).

½ cup (125 mL): 139 Calories; 5.2 g Total Fat; 470 mg Sodium; 9 g Protein; 15 g Carbohydrate; 2 g Dietary Fiber

VEGETABLE PIZZA SAUCE

Smooth reddish orange sauce. Mild spicy flavor.

Chopped onion	1 cup	250 mL
Garlic clove, minced	1	1
(or $1/4$ tsp., 1 mL, garlic powder)		
Medium tomatoes, chopped	4	4
Small green pepper, chopped	1	1
Chopped carrot	$1/2$ cup	125 mL
Chopped celery	$1/2$ cup	125 mL
Chopped zucchini, with peel	1 cup	250 mL
Dried sweet basil	$1/2$ tsp.	2 mL
Dried whole oregano	$1/2$ tsp.	2 mL
Granulated sugar	$1/2$ tsp.	2 mL
Parsley flakes	$1/2$ tsp.	2 mL
Seasoning salt	1 tsp.	5 mL
Pepper	$1/8$ tsp.	0.5 mL
Vegetable bouillon powder	1 tsp.	5 mL

Measure all 14 ingredients into blender. Process until smooth. This is easier to do by processing a few ingredients, then adding a few more, continuing until all have been added. Transfer to medium saucepan. Bring vegetable mixture to a boil. Boil slowly for 1 to $1 1/4$ hours, stirring often, until thickened. Makes 2 cups (500 mL).

$1/2$ cup (125 mL): 67 Calories; 0.7 g Total Fat; 521 mg Sodium; 3 g Protein; 15 g Carbohydrate; 4 g Dietary Fiber

GARDEN TOMATO PIZZA SAUCE

When your garden is full of tomatoes, make lots of this to keep on hand. Chunky reddish sauce. Freezes well. Delicious on Meaty Pizza Special, page 139.

Cooking oil	1 tbsp.	15 mL
Garlic cloves, minced (or $1/2$ tsp.,	2	2
2 mL, garlic powder)		
Finely chopped onion	2 cups	500 mL
Chopped tomato (2 lbs., 900 g)	$5 1/2$ cups	1.4 L
Ketchup	2 tbsp.	30 mL
Dried sweet basil	1 tsp.	5 mL
Parsley flakes	1 tsp.	5 mL
Granulated sugar	$1/2$ tsp.	2 mL
Salt	$1/2$ tsp.	2 mL
Pepper	$1/8$ tsp.	0.5 mL

(continued on next page)

Heat cooking oil in medium saucepan. Add garlic and onion. Sauté until soft and clear.

Add remaining 7 ingredients. Stir together. Bring to a boil. Boil gently for 30 to 40 minutes, stirring occasionally, until thickened. Boil longer if you want it to be thicker. Makes 3½ cups (875 mL).

½ cup (125 mL): 68 Calories; 2.5 g Total Fat; 265 mg Sodium; 2 g Protein; 12 g Carbohydrate; 2 g Dietary Fiber

MARINARA PIZZA SAUCE

Red, thick, chunky and spiced just right. Try on Sausage Coin Pizza, page 145, or S'Getti And Meatball Pizza, page 28.

Olive (or cooking) oil	1 tbsp.	15 mL
Chopped onion	1 cup	250 mL
Garlic clove, minced (or ¼ tsp., 1 mL, garlic powder)	1	1
Canned tomatoes, with juice, broken up	19 oz.	540 mL
Tomato paste	5½ oz.	156 mL
Dried sweet basil	½ tsp.	2 mL
Dried whole oregano	¼ tsp.	1 mL
Salt	½ tsp.	2 mL
Pepper	⅛ tsp.	0.5 mL
Granulated sugar	1 tsp.	5 mL
Sliced fresh mushrooms	2 cups	500 mL
White (or alcohol-free white) wine	1½ tbsp.	25 mL

Heat olive oil in large saucepan. Add onion and garlic. Sauté until soft.

Add next 7 ingredients. Heat, stirring often, until boiling. Boil gently for about 15 minutes.

Add mushrooms. Stir together. Boil for 10 minutes.

Stir in wine. Makes 3 cups (750 mL).

½ cup (125 mL): 87 Calories; 2.9 g Total Fat; 396 mg Sodium; 3 g Protein; 14 g Carbohydrate; 3 g Dietary Fiber

FAVORITE TOMATO PIZZA SAUCE

Slightly chunky from onion. Good flavor without being strong. A fast and tasty favorite for many.

Chopped onion	1 cup	250 mL
Garlic clove, minced (or ¼ tsp., 1 mL, garlic powder)	1	1
Water	½ cup	125 mL
Condensed tomato soup	10 oz.	284 mL
White vinegar	2 tbsp.	30 mL
Bay leaf	1	1
Dried sweet basil	1 tsp.	5 mL
Dried whole oregano	½ tsp.	2 mL
Parsley flakes	½ tsp.	2 mL
Chopped chives	1 tsp.	5 mL
Ground thyme, just a pinch		
Salt	¼ tsp.	1 mL
Pepper	⅛ tsp.	0.5 mL
Granulated sugar	¼ tsp.	1 mL

Cook onion and garlic in water in medium saucepan until soft. Do not drain.

Add remaining 11 ingredients. Stir together. Bring to a boil. Boil slowly for about 15 minutes until thickened. Add a touch of water if too thick. Discard bay leaf. Makes 1½ cups (375 mL).

½ cup (125 mL): 96 Calories; 1.7 g Total Fat; 927 mg Sodium; 2 g Protein; 20 g Carbohydrate; 2 g Dietary Fiber

Police made a quick trip to the chip shop. They got a tip that the fish were being battered.

MEATY PIZZA SPECIAL

Good combination of meat and cheese. Very flavorful. You might want a knife and fork to eat this one.

Pizza crust dough, your choice, pages 115 to 130	1	1
Beef sirloin steak strips	¼ lb.	113 g
Cooking oil	1 tsp.	5 mL
Garden Tomato Pizza Sauce, page 136 (or other)	½ cup	125 mL
Grated part-skim mozzarella cheese	¾ cup	175 mL
Thinly sliced pepperoni	½ cup	125 mL
Diced cooked ham	½ cup	125 mL
Grated medium Cheddar cheese	½ cup	125 mL
Grated part-skim mozzarella cheese	½ cup	125 mL

Prepare pizza dough. Roll out and press in greased 12 inch (30 cm) pizza pan, forming rim around edge.

Stir-fry beef strips in cooking oil in medium non-stick frying pan until desired doneness.

Spread sauce over crust. Sprinkle with first amount of mozzarella cheese. Scatter prepared beef, pepperoni and ham over top.

Toss Cheddar cheese and second amount of mozzarella cheese together in small bowl. Sprinkle over meat. Bake on bottom rack in 425°F (220°C) oven for 15 to 20 minutes, or for 10 minutes if using partially baked crust. Cuts into 8 wedges.

1 wedge: 326 Calories; 15.8 g Total Fat; 575 mg Sodium; 17 g Protein; 28 g Carbohydrate; 1 g Dietary Fiber

SAUSAGE PIZZA

A light golden pizza. Very tasty.

Basic Pizza Crust dough, page 115 (or other)	1	1
Sausage meat	1 lb.	454 g
Chopped onion	1 cup	250 mL
Basic Pizza Sauce, page 132 (or other)	½ cup	125 mL
Grated Edam (or mozzarella) cheese	¾ cup	175 mL
Grated part-skim mozzarella cheese	¾ cup	175 mL
Grated Parmesan cheese, sprinkle		

Prepare pizza dough. Roll out and press in greased 12 inch (30 cm) pizza pan, forming rim around edge.

Scramble-fry sausage meat and onion in medium frying pan until meat is no longer pink. Drain well.

Add pizza sauce. Stir together.

Sprinkle Edam cheese over crust. Spoon meat mixture over top. Sprinkle with mozzarella cheese and Parmesan cheese. Bake on bottom rack in 425°F (220°C) oven for about 15 minutes, or for about 8 minutes if using partially baked crust. Cuts into 8 wedges.

1 wedge: 342 Calories; 18.5 g Total Fat; 535 mg Sodium; 13 g Protein; 30 g Carbohydrate; 2 g Dietary Fiber

TROPICAL PLEASURE PIZZA

Bacon, ricotta cheese and pineapple are combined for a colorful and great tasting effect.

Pizza crust dough, your choice, pages 115 to 130	1	1
Bacon slices, diced	8	8
Basic Pizza Sauce, page 132 (or other)	½ cup	125 mL
Grated part-skim mozzarella cheese	¾ cup	175 mL
Part-skim ricotta cheese	1 cup	250 mL
Canned pineapple tidbits, drained	8 oz.	227 mL
Grated part-skim mozzarella cheese	¾ cup	175 mL

(continued on next page)

Prepare pizza dough. Roll out and press in greased 12 inch (30 cm) pizza pan, forming rim around edge.

Cook bacon in medium frying pan. Drain.

Spread pizza sauce over crust. Sprinkle with first amount of mozzarella cheese. Place dabs of ricotta cheese here and there. Scatter bacon over top. Arrange pineapple over bacon. Sprinkle second amount of mozzarella cheese over all. Bake on bottom rack in 425°F (220°C) oven for 20 to 25 minutes, or for about 15 minutes if using partially baked crust. Cuts into 8 wedges.

1 wedge: 309 Calories; 13.3 g Total Fat; 409 mg Sodium; 15 g Protein; 32 g Carbohydrate; 2 g Dietary Fiber

BACON PIZZA

Simply bacon and cheese flavor. Quick and easy.

Pizza crust dough, your choice, pages 115 to 130	1	1
Canadian back bacon slices	12	12
Favorite Tomato Pizza Sauce, page 138 (or other)	½ cup	125 mL
Grated part-skim mozzarella cheese	¾ cup	175 mL
Grated part-skim mozzarella cheese	¾ cup	175 mL

Prepare pizza dough. Roll out and press in greased 12 inch (30 cm) pizza pan, forming rim around edge.

Spray medium non-stick frying pan with cooking spray. Cook bacon quickly. Drain. Cut into nickel-size pieces.

Spread sauce over crust. Sprinkle with first amount of cheese. Scatter bacon over cheese. Sprinkle with second amount of cheese. Bake on bottom rack in 425°F (220°C) oven for 15 to 20 minutes, or for about 9 minutes if using partially baked crust. Cuts into 8 wedges.

1 wedge: 287 Calories; 10.6 g Total Fat; 848 mg Sodium; 18 g Protein; 29 g Carbohydrate; 1 g Dietary Fiber

THREE MEAT PIZZA

With a complementary mustard base, it is hard to decide which has the priority, color or taste.

Pizza crust dough, your choice, pages 115 to 130	1	1
Bacon slices	4	4
Light salad dressing (or mayonnaise)	⅓ cup	75 mL
Prepared mustard	1 tbsp.	15 mL
Thinly sliced salami, cut up	½ cup	125 mL
Thinly sliced pepperoni	½ cup	125 mL
Grated part-skim mozzarella cheese	1 cup	250 mL
Grated Parmesan cheese	2 tbsp.	30 mL

Prepare pizza dough. Roll out and press in greased 12 inch (30 cm) pizza pan, forming rim around edge.

Cook bacon slices in medium frying pan. Drain. Cut into ½ inch (12 mm) pieces. You should have about ½ cup (125 mL).

Stir salad dressing and mustard together in small cup. Spread over crust. Sprinkle bacon over top.

Sprinkle remaining 4 ingredients over bacon in order given. Bake on bottom rack in 425°F (220°C) oven for 15 to 20 minutes, or for about 10 minutes if using partially baked crust. Cheese should be browned slightly and "puffed." Cuts into 8 wedges.

1 wedge: 317 Calories; 16.9 g Total Fat; 630 mg Sodium; 12 g Protein; 28 g Carbohydrate; 1 g Dietary Fiber

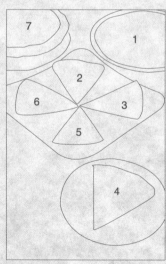

1. Macaroni Pizza, page 114
2. Tamale Pizza, page 38
3. Hamburger Pizza, page 40
4. Tomato Broccoli Pizza, page 112
   (on Wheat Biscuit Pizza Crust)
5. Jambalaya Pizza, page 97
   (on Basic Pizza Crust)
6. Stew Stuffed Pizza, page 94
7. Garden Pizza, page 104
   (on Confetti Biscuit Pizza Crust)

Props Courtesy Of: The Bay

A real favorite. So tasty and colorful with golden cheese on top.

Basic Pizza Crust dough, page 115 (or other)	1	1
Cooking oil	2 tsp.	10 mL
Small onion, cut in half lengthwise and thinly sliced	1	1
Small green pepper, thinly sliced	1	1
Marinara Pizza Sauce, page 137 (or other)	½ cup	125 mL
Grated part-skim mozzarella cheese	½ cup	125 mL
Frozen precooked sausage, thawed, sliced ¼ inch (6 mm) thick	5 oz.	140 g
Sliced fresh mushrooms	1 cup	250 mL
Grated part-skim mozzarella cheese	½ cup	125 mL
Grated medium Cheddar cheese	½ cup	125 mL

Prepare pizza dough. Roll out and press in greased 12 inch (30 cm) pizza pan, forming rim around edge.

Heat cooking oil in medium frying pan. Add onion and green pepper. Sauté until tender-crisp.

Spread sauce over crust. Sprinkle with first amount of mozzarella cheese. Scatter green pepper mixture over cheese. Arrange sausage pieces over top. Arrange mushrooms over sausage.

Toss second amount of mozzarella cheese and Cheddar cheese together in small bowl. Sprinkle over mushrooms. Bake on bottom rack in 425°F (220°C) oven for about 15 minutes, or for about 10 minutes if using partially baked crust. Cuts into 8 wedges.

1 wedge: 319 Calories; 16.6 g Total Fat; 395 mg Sodium; 12 g Protein; 30 g Carbohydrate; 2 g Dietary Fiber

Paré Pointer

If you have an automobile and a candle, would you have car wax?

CHEESY SAUSAGE PIZZA

This combination is always so flavorful.

Refrigerator crescent-style rolls (8 per tube)	8 oz.	235 g
Ground sausage meat	³/₄ lb.	340 g
Chopped onion	³/₄ lb.	340 g
Basic Pizza Sauce, page 132 (or other)	¹/₂ cup	125 mL
Grated part-skim mozzarella cheese	1¹/₂ cups	375 mL
Grated Parmesan cheese	3 tbsp.	50 mL

Unroll dough. Press to fit in greased 12 inch (30 cm) pizza pan. Press seams together, forming rim around edge.

Scramble-fry sausage meat and onion in medium frying pan until onion is soft and sausage is no longer pink. Cool for 10 minutes.

Spread pizza sauce over crust. Spread sausage mixture over sauce.

Sprinkle with mozzarella cheese and Parmesan cheese. Bake on bottom rack in 375°F (190°C) oven for about 13 minutes. Cuts into 8 wedges.

1 wedge: 318 Calories; 24.1 g Total Fat; 652 mg Sodium; 13 g Protein; 12 g Carbohydrate; 1 g Dietary Fiber

CHEESY SAUSAGE TORTILLAS: Use four 8 inch (20 cm) flour tortillas. Divide topping among them. Bake on ungreased baking sheets as above but for only about 5 minutes.

Paré Pointer

If you've been growling all day you will be dog tired at night.

CHICKEN CAESAR SALAD PIZZA

Like a chicken Caesar salad on bread. More chicken may be added if desired.

Biscuit Pizza Crust dough, page 128 (or Biscuit Mix Pizza Crust dough, page 129)	1	1
Cooking oil	1 tsp.	5 mL
Boneless, skinless chicken breast halves (about 2), sliced or slivered	½ lb.	225 g
Salt, sprinkle		
Pepper, sprinkle		
Light creamy Caesar dressing	½ cup	125 mL
Grated part-skim mozzarella cheese	¾ cup	175 mL
Finely chopped Romaine lettuce	2 cups	500 mL
Light creamy Caesar dressing	¼ cup	60 mL
Grated Parmesan cheese	3 tbsp.	50 mL

Prepare pizza dough. Roll out and press in greased 12 inch (30 cm) pizza pan, forming rim around edge.

Place cooking oil and chicken in medium non-stick frying pan. Sprinkle with salt and pepper. Sauté for about 5 minutes until chicken is cooked.

Spread first amount of Caesar dressing over crust. Sprinkle mozzarella cheese over dressing. Scatter chicken over top. Bake on bottom rack in 425°F (220°C) oven for 13 to 15 minutes, or for 8 minutes if using partially baked crust.

Toss lettuce with second amount of Caesar dressing in large bowl. Spoon over top.

Sprinkle with Parmesan cheese. Serve hot. Cuts into 8 wedges.

1 wedge: 265 Calories; 9.2 g Total Fat; 453 mg Sodium; 14 g Protein; 31 g Carbohydrate; 2 g Dietary Fiber

Pictured on page 89.

MERRY-GO-ROUND SALAD PIZZA

This pretty pizza will remind you of a Cobb salad. A knife and fork may be used if desired. Have your crust baked and other ingredients ready. Assemble shortly before serving to prevent sogginess.

Biscuit Pizza Crust dough, page 128 (or Biscuit Mix Pizza Crust dough, page 129)	1	1
Light cream cheese, softened	4 oz.	125 g
Non-fat sour cream	¼ cup	60 mL
Blue cheese, softened and mashed	2 tbsp.	30 mL
Onion powder	⅛ tsp.	0.5 mL
Hard-boiled eggs	3	3
Pimiento-stuffed green olives, sliced	14	14
Sliced small fresh mushrooms	1 cup	250 mL
Large avocado, diced	1	1
Juice of 1 lemon		
Tomatoes, diced	2	2

Prepare pizza dough. Roll out and press in greased 12 inch (30 cm) pizza pan, forming rim around edge. Bake on bottom rack in 400°F (205°C) oven for 10 to 15 minutes to cook through. Cool.

Combine next 4 ingredients in small bowl. Beat together. Spread over crust.

Cut hard-boiled eggs in half. Grate whites into small bowl. Grate or sieve yolks into separate small bowl. Spoon yolks onto center of pizza. Surround with whites.

Surround whites with olives. Make a ring of mushrooms around olives. Toss avocado in lemon juice and make a ring around mushrooms followed by a ring of tomato. Cuts into 8 wedges.

*1 **wedge:** 277 Calories; 12.8 g Total Fat; 446 mg Sodium; 9 g Protein; 33 g Carbohydrate; 3 g Dietary Fiber*

Pictured on page 71.

It's a smart mother-in-law who has lots to say but remains wordless.

Very pretty! Lots of color and texture.

Refrigerator crescent-style rolls (8 per tube)	**8 oz.**	**235 g**
Non-fat spreadable cream cheese	**4 oz.**	**113 g**
Light salad dressing (or mayonnaise)	**¼ cup**	**60 mL**
Non-fat sour cream	**¼ cup**	**60 mL**
Envelope ranch-style salad dressing mix	**½ × 1 oz.**	**½ × 28 g**
Cauliflower florets, coarsely chopped	**⅔ cup**	**150 mL**
Broccoli florets, coarsely chopped	**⅔ cup**	**150 mL**
Grated carrot	**½ cup**	**125 mL**
Small (or large, sliced) fresh mushrooms	**1 cup**	**250 mL**
Grated or very thinly sliced red pepper	**⅓ cup**	**75 mL**
Finely chopped green onion	**3 tbsp.**	**50 mL**
Grated medium Cheddar cheese (optional)	**½ cup**	**125 mL**

Sliced pitted ripe olives, for garnish
Thinly sliced tomato, for garnish

Unroll dough. Press to fit in greased 12 inch (30 cm) pizza pan. Press seams together to seal. Bake on bottom rack in 375°F (190°C) oven for 10 minutes. Cool.

Stir next 4 ingredients together in small bowl. Spread over crust.

Scatter next 7 ingredients over top in order given.

Garnish with olives and tomato. Chill. Cuts into 8 wedges.

1 wedge: 119 Calories; 5.5 g Total Fat; 393 mg Sodium; 3 g Protein; 15 g Carbohydrate; 1 g Dietary Fiber

Pictured on front cover.

Let's be like chickens. Let's start a race from scratch.

CRAB LOUIS SALAD PIZZA

Have your crust baked and other ingredients ready. Assemble just before serving to prevent sogginess. Serve with a knife and fork.

Pizza crust dough, your choice, pages 115 to 130	1	1
Light salad dressing (or mayonnaise)	½ cup	125 mL
Chili sauce	¼ cup	60 mL
Finely chopped green pepper (optional)	2 tbsp.	30 mL
Chopped green onion	⅓ cup	75 mL
Lemon juice	1 tsp.	5 mL
Worcestershire sauce	½ tsp.	2 mL
Chopped head lettuce, lightly packed	3 cups	750 mL
Canned crabmeat, drained and cartilage removed	2 x 4 oz.	2 x 113 g
Cherry tomatoes, quartered	6	6
Large hard-boiled eggs, each cut into 6 wedges	4	4
Pepper, sprinkle		
Light salad dressing (or mayonnaise)	3 tbsp.	50 mL
Milk	1 tbsp.	15 mL
Paprika, sprinkle		

Prepare pizza dough. Roll out and press in greased 12 inch (30 cm) pizza pan, forming rim around edge. Poke holes all over yeast dough with fork. If using biscuit dough, no need to poke holes. Bake on bottom rack in 425°F (220°C) oven for 10 to 12 minutes. Press down any bulges in yeast dough with tea towel. Cool.

Mix next 6 ingredients in small bowl. Spread over crust.

Sprinkle lettuce over top.

Scatter crabmeat, tomato and egg wedges over top. Tomato and egg can be scattered randomly or placed on each slice. Sprinkle with pepper.

Stir second amount of salad dressing and milk together in small cup. Drizzle over all.

Sprinkle with paprika. Cuts into 8 wedges.

1 wedge: 274 Calories; 11 g Total Fat; 557 mg Sodium; 11 g Protein; 32 g Carbohydrate; 2 g Dietary Fiber

Pictured on page 125.

MEASUREMENT TABLES

Throughout this book measurements are given in Conventional and Metric measure. To compensate for differences between the two measurements due to rounding, a full metric measure is not always used. The cup used is the standard 8 fluid ounce. Temperature is given in degrees Fahrenheit and Celsius. Baking pan measurements are in inches and centimetres as well as quarts and litres. An exact metric conversion is given below as well as the working equivalent (Standard Measure).

OVEN TEMPERATURES

Fahrenheit (°F)	Celsius (°C)
175°	80°
200°	95°
225°	110°
250°	120°
275°	140°
300°	150°
325°	160°
350°	175°
375°	190°
400°	205°
425°	220°
450°	230°
475°	240°
500°	260°

SPOONS

Conventional Measure	Metric Exact Conversion Millilitre (mL)	Metric Standard Measure Millilitre (mL)
1/8 teaspoon (tsp.)	0.6 mL	0.5 mL
1/4 teaspoon (tsp.)	1.2 mL	1 mL
1/2 teaspoon (tsp.)	2.4 mL	2 mL
1 teaspoon (tsp.)	4.7 mL	5 mL
2 teaspoons (tsp.)	9.4 mL	10 mL
1 tablespoon (tbsp.)	14.2 mL	15 mL

CUPS

	Metric Exact Conversion Millilitre (mL)	Metric Standard Measure Millilitre (mL)
1/4 cup (4 tbsp.)	56.8 mL	60 mL
1/3 cup (5 1/3 tbsp.)	75.6 mL	75 mL
1/2 cup (8 tbsp.)	113.7 mL	125 mL
2/3 cup (10 2/3 tbsp.)	151.2 mL	150 mL
3/4 cup (12 tbsp.)	170.5 mL	175 mL
1 cup (16 tbsp.)	227.3 mL	250 mL
4 1/2 cups	1022.9 mL	1000 mL (1 L)

PANS

Conventional Inches	Metric Centimetres
8x8 inch	20x20 cm
9x9 inch	22x22 cm
9x13 inch	22x33 cm
10x15 inch	25x38 cm
11x17 inch	28x43 cm
8x2 inch round	20x5 cm
9x2 inch round	22x5 cm
10x4 1/2 inch tube	25x11 cm
8x4x3 inch loaf	20x10x7.5 cm
9x5x3 inch loaf	22x12.5x7.5 cm

DRY MEASUREMENTS

Conventional Measure Ounces (oz.)	Metric Exact Conversion Grams (g)	Metric Standard Measure Grams (g)
1 oz.	28.3 g	28 g
2 oz.	56.7 g	57 g
3 oz.	85.0 g	85 g
4 oz.	113.4 g	125 g
5 oz.	141.7 g	140 g
6 oz.	170.1 g	170 g
7 oz.	198.4 g	200 g
8 oz.	226.8 g	250 g
16 oz.	453.6 g	500 g
32 oz.	907.2 g	1000 g (1 kg)

CASSEROLES (Canada & Britain)

Standard Size Casserole	Exact Metric Measure
1 qt. (5 cups)	1.13 L
1 1/2 qts. (7 1/2 cups)	1.69 L
2 qts. (10 cups)	2.25 L
2 1/2 qts. (12 1/2 cups)	2.81 L
3 qts. (15 cups)	3.38 L
4 qts. (20 cups)	4.5 L
5 qts. (25 cups)	5.63 L

CASSEROLES (United States)

Standard Size Casserole	Exact Metric Measure
1 qt. (4 cups)	900 mL
1 1/2 qts. (6 cups)	1.35 L
2 qts. (8 cups)	1.8 L
2 1/2 qts. (10 cups)	2.25 L
3 qts. (12 cups)	2.7 L
4 qts. (16 cups)	3.6 L
5 qts. (20 cups)	4.5 L

INDEX

Mail Order Form

See reverse for list of cookbooks

EXCLUSIVE MAIL ORDER OFFER
Buy 2 Get 1 FREE!
Buy any 2 cookbooks—choose a **3rd FREE** of equal or less value than the lowest price paid.

QUANTITY	CODE	TITLE	PRICE EACH	PRICE TOTAL
			$	$
	TOTAL BOOKS (including FREE)			

DON'T FORGET to indicate your FREE book(s). (see exclusive mail order offer above)

PLEASE PRINT

TOTAL BOOKS PURCHASED: $

	INTERNATIONAL		CANADA & USA	
Plus Shipping & Handling (PER DESTINATION)	$ 7.00	(one book)	$ 5.00	(1-3 books)
Additional Books (INCLUDING FREE BOOKS)	$	($2.00 each)	$	($1.00 each)
SUB-TOTAL	$		$	
Canadian residents add G.S.T (7%)			$	
TOTAL AMOUNT ENCLOSED	$		$	

The Fine Print
- Orders outside Canada must be **PAID IN US FUNDS** by cheque or money order drawn on Canadian or US bank or by credit card.
- Make cheque or money order payable to: **COMPANY'S COMING PUBLISHING LIMITED.**
- Prices are expressed in Canadian dollars for Canada, US dollars for USA & International and are subject to change without prior notice.
- Orders are shipped surface mail. For courier rates, visit our web-site: **www.companyscoming.com** or contact us: **Tel: (780) 450-6223 Fax: (780) 450-1857.**
- Sorry, no C.O.D's.

☐ MasterCard   ☐ VISA

Expiry date

Account #

Name of cardholder

Cardholder's signature

Shipping Address
Send the cookbooks listed above to:

Name:

Street:

City: _____ Prov./State:

Country: _____ Postal Code/Zip:

Tel: ( )

E-mail address:

Gift Giving
- Let us help you with your gift giving!
- We will send cookbooks directly to the recipients of your choice if you give us their names and addresses.
- Please specify the titles you wish to send to each person.
- If you would like to include your personal note or card, we will be pleased to enclose it with your gift order.
- Company's Coming Cookbooks make excellent gifts: Birthdays, bridal showers, Mother's Day, Father's Day, graduation or any occasion... collect them all!

Company's Coming cookbooks are available
at retail locations *THROUGHOUT* Canada!

See reverse for mail order

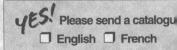

Sample Recipe from
One-Dish Meals
Chicken Fajita Dinner

Everyone in the family will like this one.
A very child-friendly meal.

Lime juice	2 tbsp.	30 mL
Garlic cloves, minced (or ½ tsp., 2 mL) powder	2	2
Dried crushed chilies, finely crushed	¼ tsp.	1 mL
Salt	¼ tsp.	1 mL
Pepper, sprinkle		
Boneless, skinless chicken breast halves (about 4), cut into thin strips	1 lb.	454 g
Cooking oil	2 tsp.	10 mL
Small or medium mild red (or white) onions, sliced and separated into rings	2	2
Medium red pepper, slivered	1	1
Medium green or yellow pepper, slivered	1	1
Frozen kernel corn, thawed	1 cup	250 mL
Medium chunky salsa	1 cup	250 mL
Water	2 tsp.	10 mL
Cornstarch	1 tsp.	5 mL
Corn chips, optional	8½ oz.	250 g

Put first 5 ingredients into medium bowl. Stir together well. Add chicken strips. Stir together. Cover. Marinate in refrigerator for 1 to 2 hours.

Heat cooking oil in large frying pan. Add chicken and marinade. Stir-fry for about 3 minutes.

Add onion and peppers. Stir together. Cover. Cook for about 4 minutes, stirring occasionally.

Add corn and salsa. Stir together. Cook, uncovered, stirring occasionally, until hot and bubbling.

Mix water and cornstarch in small cup. Stir into boiling mixture until thickened.

Sprinkle with corn chips or stir them in. They will stay crisp for about 15 minutes if stirred in. Serves 4.

1 serving: 219 Calories; 3.9 g Total Fat; 1128 mg Sodium; 27 g Protein; 23 g Carbohydrate; 3 g Dietary Fiber